Adamant
FAITH

CLINGING TO AN

UNSHAKABLE GOD

IN AN EVER-CHANGING WORLD

Bridging THE *Gap*

To Tiffany Wendt, who chose to courageously worship God through the pain of cancer, declaring "it is my honor." Though Tiffany is now pain-free, it's our turn and our honor to worship God through the pain of grieving.

Tiffany faced her fears and always maintained that "God is God and God is good"—despite what her medical reports would say. She lived a life filled with tenacious hope and adamant faith, and her trust was in the Lord.

As followers of Jesus Christ, we do grieve; but we grieve differently. We grieve with hope (1 Thessalonians 4:13).

Tiffany Wendt
(1981–2019)

Contents

Section 3: Adamant Faith Inspires Me To...

Introduction

Unswerving. Resolute. Unyielding.

I am convinced about Jesus: His goodness, kindness, promises, mercy, and plan.

In a world that is constantly shifting, I am more certain than ever of our need to stand firm on Truth—the Rock that is Jesus.

Adamant Faith is steady and unrelenting. It is a stronghold and anchor. It believes God fiercely and won't back down. If he said it, he means it. He won't give up on me, so I won't give up on him.

I believe prayer is the key! Prayer is the way we take our hands off and let God put his hands on. Prayer is the difference between you fighting for God and God fighting for you.

The writer of Psalm 35:23 understands: "Contend for me, my God and Lord." So does author Mark Batterson: "It refers to both physical combat and verbal combat. God is like a mother grizzly that protects her cubs. It is God's instinctive nature because we are the 'apple of His eye.' If anyone messes with us, they are messing with the Father."

Behind the scenes, we have two intercessors. The Holy Spirit intercedes on our behalf; long after we go to sleep he circles us in prayer. And the Son of God is circling us *always* with words of deliverance.

There is more on the horizon if we dare take steps to believe him—but it takes Adamant Faith to start walking and keep walking, our footing placed with assurance on this solid foundation.

My desire for you is to take the challenge. He is with you always! "The Lord is my rock, my fortress, and my deliverer . . . my stronghold" (Psalm 18:2). And my prayer for you is that you never forget it.

Carol Lund
Director, Bridging the Gap

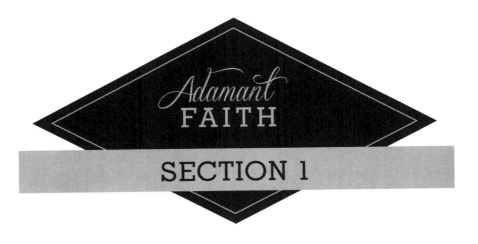

SECTION 1

Adamant Faith is
Anchored in...

Day 1

Adamant Faith is Anchored in
Replacing Lies With Truth

SUSIE LARSON

In my distress I prayed to the Lord,
and the Lord answered me and set me free.

Psalm 118:5 (NLT)

I've struggled with fear my whole life, and I never thought I'd be free of it. But now I know differently. It is *for freedom* that Christ has set us free.

God will allow an overplayed enemy attack when he knows we're ready and strong enough to win the battle for our freedom. That's what happened to me with my recent health battle.

Like a weed that sneakily surfaced in my yard, I realized that this fear had its roots in me. My health relapse brought up old symptoms and brand-new ones. It felt like Satan had launched another *new* attack on my life. Yet I'd soon learn that this current threat was indeed connected to an old fear. Though it seemed like God had done nothing to stop the enemy's threats against me, I realized once again that he has a purpose for everything he does. He is 100 percent committed, involved, and purposeful in everything he allows into our lives. He only allowed me to be stirred up because he had determined that it was time for me to be free.

My husband serves on the board of a ministry that serves the people in Rwanda. At the end of his first trip, the team went on a safari. He came home and said,

"I learned something about lions. They have a loud roar and they're fast but only for a distance. They don't have endurance. That's why they rely on their ability to prowl, strategize, and intimidate."

> *"Stay alert! Watch out for your great enemy, the devil. He prowls around like a roaring lion, looking for someone to devour. Stand firm against him and be strong in your faith. Remember that your family of believers all over the world is going through the same kind of suffering you are."*
>
> *1 Peter 5:8–9 (NLT)*

In other words, the fear-lion slinks around in the shadows. He relies on surprise attacks and his loud roar. The fear-lion prowls around and looks for an opening in our lives. At best, he wants to disrupt our peace; at worst, he hopes to bait us into sin, ruin our lives, and rob us of our influence, perspective, and joy.

Our fear gives Satan a geographical presence that he doesn't deserve.[1]

The scrawny, emaciated fear-lion finds an opening in our lives where he knows he's already planted fear. He knows us well. He's studied us for years. He remembers well the traps he set for us when we were just children. He knows what lies he fed us when life let us down. He watches our response to certain triggers. And as long as we react to our fears instead of responding to God's promises, the enemy's strategy against us will continually be successful.

But fear is a liar. The enemy is a liar. He's the author of confusion. And his threat against us is directly connected to our threat to him. Consider the way the enemy relentlessly comes against you. Now turn it around and ponder what mind-boggling call God has in mind for you! Yes, you need healing to walk out this calling. But don't we all?

---

1 Nik Ripken (pseudonym). Expert on the persecuted church.

Jesus knows the layers of your pain, hurts, and traumas. And he knows exactly how to unearth them without destroying you. He's wonderfully careful with you. And he's ruthless with your enemy. He will in due time heal and restore you. And make no mistake about it. He will also destroy the works of the enemy in your life.

Remember, the devil fights dirty. And life is just plain hard sometimes. Even so, may we stay determined and grab hold of this truth: *God has made promises to us that he intends to keep.*

Let's fight for our freedom so we can know the flourishing Jesus offers us. When we flourish, others flourish as well. Our life, our freedom matters so very much in the greater Kingdom story. We can do this.

Reflect And Respond

What is your current battle stirring up in you? What's God saying to you?

_____

_____

_____

Does this feel like a new threat connected to an old lie?

_____

_____

_____

Susie Larson is a national speaker, radio host, and author. She's a wife, mother, and grandmother to two adorable grandchildren.

Adapted from Susie Larson's book Fully Alive: Learning to Flourish, Mind, Body, and Spirit *(Bethany House Publishers, 2018). Used with permission.*

Day 2

Adamant Faith is Anchored in
Balancing Truth and Love

LISA BEVERE

Instead, we will speak the truth in love,
growing in every way more and more like Christ,
who is the head of his body, the church.

Ephesians 4:15 (NLT)

Walk into most churches nowadays and you will likely hear a message of love, hope, and encouragement. And all that is good and well. After years of overly harsh messages, the pendulum has naturally swung to the other side—but have we swung it too far? Are we so set on being seeker-friendly that we neglect what it means to be a true friend to those walking through our doors?

The mistake we made in past decades was to tell the truth in insensitive ways. The answer to this is not to shrink back from speaking truth. It is to learn to speak the truth *in love.*

Jesus was certainly a friend of sinners—and we should be too—but it's time we reassess what being a friend looks like. I, for one, expect my friends to tell me the truth. I don't want them to bash me over the head with it, but I do want them to tell me the things I need to hear in a loving manner.

We've all been given truth without love at times. It's not fun. Truth without love is mean—but love without truth is meaningless. We need both. When we look at Jesus, we see these two qualities on full display. He is the God who so loved the world. He is love itself. Yet he is also the truth (John 14:6).

Consider the example of the woman caught in adultery in John chapter 8. She is exposed in her sin and is surrounded by her self-righteous accusers who want to stone her. Jesus reaches down and writes something mysterious in the sand. Then he stands up and says, "Let any one of you who is without sin be the first to throw a stone at her." One by one, beginning with the older ones, her accusers turn away. And then comes grace. Jesus turns to her and says, "Woman, where are they? Has no one condemned you?" She responds, "No one, sir." And he says, "Then neither do I condemn you."

What an amazing embodiment of grace on full display. The God of eternity reached down into the dust of her existence and transformed it in a moment.

But if Jesus had the attitude of most churches today, that's where the story would end. Thankfully, his adamant love for us extends beyond that. As beautiful as the words "Then neither do I condemn you" are, his next words are equally loving. He tells her, "Go now and leave your life of sin."

Why? Because he knows she's been looking for life in places she can't find it. Because he sees the broken ways of living she's embraced and in his love, he calls her to leave them behind. He sees the pain her choices have caused both her and others, and he has much better things in store.

Do you see this?

Jesus's call is not condemning. He's inviting her to *more*—and it's breathtakingly beautiful. You see, Jesus loves us where we are, but he never leaves us where we are. He calls us into life.

My question is, as a church, are we doing the same?

It is not God's Word that is silent on the controversial topics of our day—it's us. We are not truly loving people the way Jesus did if we shy back from truth under the guise of love. Jesus never did this. His love runs so much deeper than that.

Beloved, let's be like Jesus, full of compassion, yet adamant in truth.

May we never cease to declare with boldness the unchanging, constant, unconditional, infinite, undeserved, adamant love of God—but let's remember that love always calls us out of brokenness into something better.

Let's never forget that the same Jesus who says, "Neither do I condemn you" says, "Go and leave your life of sin." He forgives us, but he also sets us free from sin's tyrannical rule in our lives and invites us into life as he intended. In his adamant love, he won't settle for anything less.

Reflect and Respond

Jesus is full of grace and truth. Are you?

_____

_____

_____

Lisa Bevere has spent nearly three decades empowering women to find their identity and purpose. She is a *New York Times* bestselling author and an internationally known speaker. Her books, which include *Adamant, Without Rival, Girls with Swords,* and *Fight Like a Girl,* are in the hands of millions worldwide.

Day 3

Adamant Faith is Anchored in

Comfort in God's Care

ANDREA CHRISTENSON

He reached down from on high and took hold of me;
he drew me out of deep waters.

Psalm 18:16 (NIV)

It happened in a heartbeat. For our daughter's third birthday, the family packed up and went to a local hotel pool to swim. One moment, our three-year-old daughter stood happily splashing in the pool, laughing and calling out, "Look at me! Look at me!" In the next breath, without warning, she slipped into a spot where she couldn't touch the bottom. A look of panic spread across her face as she gulped in a huge mouthful of chlorinated water. Her arms flew up and her head slipped under the surface. During that split second, I could see her arms and legs churning as she struggled for purchase on the slippery pool tile.

My husband pulled my daughter up out of the pool within a second on that fateful birthday, and we wrapped her tightly in a towel. After many kisses and repeated reassurances, she stopped shivering and coughing. Thankfully, she was fine.

Isn't that like life sometimes? You are happily playing, without much care, when unexpected circumstances wash over you and, within a moment, you are drowning. Maybe you're facing a job loss, a health issue, or the death of a close friend. Suddenly your safe footing is no longer beneath you and life swirls around you, threatening to pull you under for good.

Perhaps, like David, you are crying out, *"The cords of death entangled me; the torrents of destruction overwhelmed me. The cords of the grave coiled around me; the snares of death confronted me"* (Psalm 18:4–5, NIV).

David's words later on in the Psalms ring true as well: *"The cords of death entangled me, the anguish of the grave came over me; I was overcome by distress and sorrow"* (Psalm 116:3). Sometimes the ground that once seemed solid shifts beneath us and we are overwhelmed by circumstances.

We visited another swimming pool a few months later. Silently, my daughter pulled on her swimsuit. Silently, she walked out onto the pool deck. But when we coaxed her to get in the pool, she steadfastly refused. She would not go in on her own. My husband picked her up and walked down the steps into the shallow end. Her little arms wrapped around his neck and held tight.

"It's alright, I've got you," he whispered into her ear. "Just hold on tight to Daddy. You will be safe." His strong arms held her close throughout their time in the pool as he constantly reassured her of his care and her safety. "Just hold on tight to Daddy."

What a beautiful picture of how God cares for us. We don't need to fear the challenges we face; instead, we can just hold tight to God. He will be our safety.

But the idea I love to think about even more is this: If my daughter had let go of her dad in that water, he would still have held her. His arms would still have kept her safe. His firm footing would have anchored her in the turbulent pool. This is true of our relationship with God as well. Sometimes we think we have to do all the grasping, be the ones to wrap our arms tight around him and his promises. Instead, God is holding on to us. His arms are a place of safety even when we can't cling any longer. God's firm footing keeps us afloat. God's love keeps us safe.

My husband's love for my daughter is powerful, but it is nothing compared to the love God exhibits for each one of us. My friends, I echo Paul's prayer from Ephesians 3:17b-19:

> *"And I pray that you, being rooted and established in love, may have power, together with all the Lord's holy people, to grasp how wide and long and high and deep is the love of Christ, and to know this love that surpasses knowledge—that you may be filled to the measure of all the fullness of God."*

May you find comfort in this all-surpassing love in the midst of life's overwhelming circumstances. May you find comfort in hearing God whisper to you, "It's alright, I've got you."

Reflect and Respond

Have you ever felt overwhelmed by the situations you find yourself in?

_____

_____

_____

What Scriptures does God whisper to your heart in times of trouble?

_____

_____

_____

Andrea Christenson is an avid coffee enthusiast, book lover, and a writer who seeks to connect to the heart of her readers and point them toward God. She lives with her husband and two daughters in western Wisconsin. You can find more information about Andrea at www.andreachristenson.com.

Day 4

Adamant Faith is Anchored in

the Word

ERICA HORZYA

Faith comes by hearing, and hearing by the word of God.
Romans 10:17 (NKJV)

It was 9:30 in the morning and my toddler was strapped to my back in the hiking backpack, as he often was when I wanted to clean the house without interruption. Standing in my kitchen, dishes piled high, that day started out like any other but ended up changing everything.

My husband and I had gotten into another fight. Adjusting to the new demands of parenthood had rocked our worlds as we struggled to navigate our new roles and synthesize our parenting philosophies. Both being strong-willed, oldest children adamantly rooted in our own ways, our relationship was badly severed. And, hatred marinating in our hearts, it was growing worse by the day. Sometimes I would hear people talk about how they had "become roommates" with their spouse and I'd think about how wonderful that sounded. Compared to the actively hostile environment we had created, just being roommates sounded like a dream.

We were in the darkest, loneliest, most difficult season of our lives.

In the kitchen that morning, still shaken by the hostility of the previous night's battle, I began to pray as I washed the dishes. I knew only God could intervene and take something so broken and make it whole. As I was praying, like I had countless times before, something new rose up inside of me. Recalling Ephesians 6:17, something finally clicked. I knew I needed to battle using the sword of the spirit—the Word of God.

I'll never forget the place I stood in my kitchen as I began speaking the promises of God aloud over my life and marriage. I was no longer simply begging for help; I was recalling and declaring every scripture I could summon about healing, wholeness, hope, and the future.

At first, I spoke through gritted teeth. The words felt like sand in my mouth. Wholeness and hope did not feel like my reality. *Did I actually believe these promises were for me? Could they make a difference in my life?*

I proceeded to wipe my counters—probably as much with tears as with water—and sing, shout, and pray God's word.

"'For I know the plans I have for you,' declares the Lord, 'plans to prosper you and not to harm you, plans to give you hope and a future,'" my weak voice cried.

That's when a boldness arose, and I grit my teeth harder, sang louder, and prayed with more authority.

"God, you said if you're for us, no one can be against us. And I know you are for me" (Romans 8:31–32).

"You said you work all things, all things, all things together for the good of those who love you" (Romans 8:28).

"There is surely a future hope for me, and my hope will not be cut off" (Proverbs 23:18).

On and on I continued to speak Scripture over my marriage. Even though I could not yet see how it would happen, I chose to believe there was breakthrough coming. Through tears of fierce determination, I adamantly took those promises and made them mine.

And that's when faith truly arose in me.

Romans 10:17 (NKJV) says, *"Faith comes by hearing, and hearing by the word of God."* Sometimes there's nothing more powerful than hearing your own voice declare his promises; it internalizes them in a whole new way. And, as James 5:16 tells us, when faith arises our prayers take on a new boldness and authority, which leads to breakthrough.

Not only did my faith emerge in a brand new way that day. There was also an undeniable breakthrough in the spiritual realm. I still don't know exactly how to describe it. When my husband arrived home after work, his heart had softened as well.

The whole tone of our household changed. It was as if an oppressive force had lifted and chains had fallen off. Not everything was perfect. It took time and work to mend our brokenness; however, there was a distinct shift in the climate of our relationship that day. The bondage of hostility and hatred that had been so prevalent in our relationship had broken. Eleven years and four more babies later, our marriage has had ebbs and flows, but I can point to that very day and that very spot in my kitchen as the moment our trajectory changed. That day I shifted from being adamantly convinced my way was right to adamantly convinced that God's Word is true—for me and my marriage.

Reflect and Respond

Are you facing a situation you're tempted to believe is too big for God? How might your actions regarding the situation change if you saw it instead as a miracle in the making?

_____

_____

_____

Read Romans 8:17. Consider whether you tend to pray as a beggar or as an heir to God's gracious promises.

_____

_____

_____

What scripture promises can you pray and declare over your situation today?

_____

_____

_____

Erica Horyza, a recovering perfectionist, is learning to embrace grace in the chaos of raising five children. She holds a B.A. from North Central University in Music, teaches fitness classes, and loves sharing her journey with other women in hopes they will embrace God's grace and draw closer to Jesus.

Day 5

Adamant Faith is Anchored in

the Heart of God

JONNA MEIDAL

"If a man has a hundred sheep and one of them wanders away,
what will he do? Won't he leave the ninety-nine others on the hills
and go out to search for the one that is lost?"

Matthew 18:12 (NLT)

The day he arrived, he was so tiny. I remember looking at his little face, wondering if I would ever learn to love him. After all, he wasn't mine. I hadn't planned for him, hadn't protected him inside my belly for nine months; yet, I had prayed for him. For years, I had prayed! And now he was here—sleeping in my living room.

God had put the burden of foster care on my heart six years prior to his arrival. But back then, he never told me what the journey would look like, or how it would feel to care for someone else's child. All he said was, "Jonna, will you go? Will you go and search for the one?"

At the time, I assumed he was talking about a child, because that's usually what I think about when I hear "foster care." Yet God had someone else in mind. He wanted me to search for my foster son's mom.

Let me pause for a second and say this was *not* what I had expected to hear. I mean, it is hard enough to love on someone who's a stranger, let alone someone who doesn't want to be found! But God's grace is way more fluid than our own, right? It can seep down into cracks and crevices no one has noticed for years. And that's exactly where he asked me to look.

I'll be honest: I didn't know if I wanted to go. I doubted my own abilities and whether I had heard God correctly, and I didn't really want to "search" for an adult either. I just wanted to love on the kids!

None of my shortcomings worried God, though. He still presented me with a choice: Would I adamantly pursue his heart or would I trust my own?

Thankfully, I chose God's path, but the road still wasn't easy. Sleepless nights, my own three children to wrangle, and countless "foster care expectations" left me feeling ragged and helpless. I cried out to Jesus almost every single day, asking for a way out, asking for him to take the pain and darkness away.

But he didn't. Not immediately, anyway. All he gave me was a vision.

He showed me climbing up a treacherous mountain, but then he lovingly added, "Jonna, you've got the oxygen tank and safety equipment to survive this journey, but you don't have *my* perspective yet. In order to get that, you don't need to know what to do; you need to know what to pray."

And then he told me to attack my fear first.

Why hadn't I thought to do this before?! After all, there is so much fear in "the system," it often feels like swimming with a bag over your head. And even though I knew that fear lurks within any unpredictable situation, rarely have I charged straight into it. But that's exactly what I did: I bulldozed into the world of foster care, unarmed—and afraid.

"As we live in God, our love grows more perfect...and such love has no fear, because perfect love expels all fear" (1 John 4:17–18, NLT).

Wow. Perfect love expels all fear! This truth hit me hard. I immediately used it to attack the darkness. I also prayed that my preconceived judgments about the birth mom would vanish and that she and I could become allies instead of foes. When I did this, the walls of fear came crashing down.

The first time I noticed this new attitude was during one of our court-mandated visits. These were usually really awkward and stressful, but on this particular day it wasn't. Somehow we managed to put our differences aside and enjoy food and laughter together, and it felt so normal!

After this experience, I heard God speak again.

"Do you see her now, Jonna?" he said. "She's a mom just like you! I left the 99 to search for her, and I need you to keep showing up on her behalf."

So I did.

Everything changed after that day. My fear was eradicated (thank you, Jesus!), and all that remained was encouragement and love. I started telling her how proud I was of her and how much I was praying for her; I also began praying that his will would be done and not mine. (After all, his ways are always higher, right?) Trusting in God's perspective is often a hard choice to make, especially when all we can see is brokenness, addiction, and abandonment. But God always sees something different, and when we choose to follow him—friends, that's when battles are won!

In the end, my foster son was able to go home and live with his mom—a woman who is now seeking God and believes 100 percent in the power of prayer! Standing in the gap for her gave me insight into what adamant faith really looks like. It has very little to do with me and how I'm feeling, and everything to do with the heart of God. And I believe his heart wants you and me to pursue "the one" more than he wants us to be comfortable and safe.

So I humbly ask you: Will you go? Will you leave the ninety-nine to search for the one? God is calling you out, my friend, and he wants his heart to become your heart.

Reflect and Respond

If God would leave the ninety-nine to search for the one, why is it so hard for us to do? What often stands in our way as Christ-followers?

_____

_____

_____

Who might God be asking you to search for? Is this person easy to find? Hard to love? Pray and reflect on what it might look like to pursue this person with the heart of God.

_____

_____

_____

Read 2 Corinthians 4:18. What might God be saying to you in this verse, especially as it applies to "the one?" Write down anything that comes to mind.

_____

_____

_____

Jonna Meidal is a mother to three girls and seeks to parent them by the fruits of the spirit. She has an M.A. in ESL and has traveled to almost 20 countries, but considers motherhood to be her greatest adventure yet! She loves laughing, dancing, and eating copious amounts of popcorn (sometimes simultaneously). Read more about her adventures at www.jonnameidal.com.

Day 6

Adamant Faith is Anchored in

God's Strength

CRYSTAL WIMPFHEIMER

The Lord is my strength and shield. I trust him with all my heart.
He helps me, and my heart is filled with joy.

Psalm 28:7 (NLT)

Hiking off the beaten path sounded fun before we started, but when my feet began to lose traction, I felt out of control. The path leading out was a steep, uphill climb covered in slick mud. In the distance, animals were scurrying and darting around. A steady stream of water at the bottom of the path provided a fresh, rain smell. Lunging forward, my hand aimed for a tree that was just out of reach but instead landed in the slimy, thick mud as my feet slid further down the hill. Lifting my sunken foot out of the mud, I took a few steps forward, gaining a few feet of ground. Reaching once again for the sturdy tree in front of me, I breathed a sigh of relief when my hand touched the rough bark. Clinging to the tree, I paused for a moment. The chirping birds, the rustling leaves, and the swooshing wind should have brought peace. Yet the goosebumps on my arms and the chill down my spine indicated another feeling: fear.

The unexpected turns and challenges of the climb that had initially brought excitement had suddenly turned into a helpless fear of the unknown. Reflecting on the feeling, I knew that I had been here before. In fact, I had faced much worse.

Just a few years ago, my marriage was falling apart. My husband was involved in another relationship, and he had a baby on the way that was not mine. Talk about sliding down a slippery, muddy mess. Those days were filled with helpless despair, my hope of a happy life far in the distance.

But on the day of my climb, even as I felt fear, I paused. Instead of feeling stuck in the mud and my own thoughts, I looked around. As I glanced up at the gorgeous array of leaves, I noticed how they were all different shades and sizes. Birds were gliding from one tree to the next. The Lord was bringing beauty and hope, even in my moments of fear.

"The Lord is my strength," I whispered to myself.

Certainly, if the Lord could pull me out of the mess in my life and put me back on solid footing, this steep hill would be nothing for him.

Our marriage unraveled when my husband and I both faced the darkness of depression and post-traumatic stress disorder. It's hard to say who experienced symptoms first, but regardless, we became trapped in our own minds, unable to escape the nightmares inside. I was so focused on my own survival that I didn't notice that my husband had begun to look beyond our marriage to cope. The day he asked for a divorce, devastation shocked my body as my mind finally woke up. During a six-month separation, I longed for hope and stability. Finding wisdom in scripture, peace through prayer, and strength even in weakness, my mind and body began to heal.

This renewal of mind and spirit led to restoration beyond anything I could have imagined. I found my identity was not in being a wife but in Christ alone. This new identity inspired me to lean into my family and my church, attend weekly individual therapy sessions, and after months of waiting started marriage counseling. Seeking the Lord's wisdom and path for my life led to reconciliation with my husband and a marriage anchored in the strength of God.

With my hand still wrapped around the tree, I took a deep breath and smelled fresh air mixed with campfire smoke. With renewed inner strength, I purposely let go of the sturdy tree and pushed forward. Up ahead, I heard heavy footsteps make their way toward where I stood. My husband came into view and reached his hand toward me, pulling me over the last section of the steep hill.

Back on flat ground, I was thankful to be out of the muddy unknown. My hand rested snugly in my husband's, and the full verse from earlier returned to mind. *"The Lord is my strength and shield. I trust him with all my heart. He helps me, and my heart is filled with joy"* (Psalm 28:7, NLT).

Through every step of life, the Lord has helped me. Even in my dark, hopeless moments, he directed my path and brought strength. When my feet were unsteady and my future uncertain, the Lord proved himself trustworthy. He replaced my fear of the unknown, giving me a heart filled with joy even in the muddy, slippery seasons of life. Our challenges are nothing compared to the strength the Lord provides when we trust in his ability.

Reflect and Respond

What steep hills in your life seem impossible right now?

_____

_____

_____

Think of a time when fear of the unknown stopped you from trusting in God's faithfulness. What helped you through that situation?

_____

_____

_____

What would it take for you to let go and depend on God's strength to help you overcome your circumstances?

_____

_____

_____

Crystal Wimpfheimer loves being a wife, mom, and social worker but has learned that her true identity comes through Christ. The Lord has used the pain in her life to demonstrate his transformative power. You can find Crystal sharing messages of hope on the mental health awareness site, www.hopeinahopelessworld.com.

Day 7

Adamant Faith is Anchored in

the One Who is Truth

ANITA MATTA

Now we see things imperfectly, like puzzling reflections in a mirror,
but then we will see everything with perfect clarity.
All that I know now is partial and incomplete, but then I will know everything
completely, just as God now knows me completely.

1 Corinthians 13:12 (NLT)

I remember a day when suddenly the whole world looked different. I was six, and I'd just been fitted with my first pair of glasses. It was the eighties, so they were as big as my face—translucent, pink, plastic beauties that have inexplicably become trendy again. But I vividly remember the immediate clarity of my world. I could read the words on the blackboard from my desk! I could see individual leaves on the trees outside my window! The world hadn't changed, but the world I could see was totally different.

Recently, the world I can see changed again, when a week before my thirty-eighth birthday a doctor finally recognized that my unexplainable lifelong health issues were actually all related to a rare genetic condition. Nearly every doctor I'd seen in my life told me there was no explanation for what I was experiencing. Many doctors told me, because all tests were normal and I looked fine, I must be depressed, the pain and debilitating weakness I was experiencing simply something my mind was convincing me was true.

That cut that wouldn't stop bleeding? I was being dramatic.

Still feeling pain at the dentist? They'd already given me extra Novacaine, so what I was feeling couldn't be pain, just pressure.

It feels like looking into a parallel universe, when I look back over my entire life through these new lenses. Suddenly I can clearly see details of my life I've never understood.

So many times, and in so many areas of life, my lenses have changed. Sometimes in small ways, revealing new details I hadn't previously noticed. Sometimes in big ways, challenging everything I thought I knew. But every time, my faith remains unchanged and unwavering.

This unwavering faith is only possible because my faith is not in my lenses, or my beliefs, but in the person of Jesus Christ.

This gives me reason to believe in a Healer even when my body is still in pain. My faith is not in healing; my faith is in the Healer.

Adamant belief in the person of Jesus, and his ultimate goodness and perfection, is what keeps me solid every time my world changes. My faith cannot be found in the glasses on my face or in the way I view the world, but in something beyond what I can see, beyond what I can understand. An unchangeable, untameable, always good, and always true father, who dearly loves me.

As Paul explained to the Corinthians, someday God will give us perfect clarity. Until then, we will peer through our imperfect lenses, with our imperfect beliefs, believing in the Truth that never changes.

Reflect and Respond

How can your prayer today be changed knowing that your belief is centered in God, The Unchangeable Truth, rather than believing in the picture you can see through your current lenses?

_____

_____

_____

Anita Matta grew up in Belize as a missionary kid. She has lived in three countries and traveled on five continents but can't resist the allure of subzero winters. She now lives in Minnesota with her Egyptian husband and two daughters. She blogs about God, motherhood, and appreciating beauty at anitamatta.com, and pretends to be trendy by posting pictures of coffee as @anitafmatta on Instagram.

Day 8

Adamant Faith is Anchored in

Being Wrecked

RHIANNON RUTLEDGE

But take courage! None of you will lose your lives,
even though the ship will go down.

Acts 27:22 (NLT)

It felt like just another day of my new normal. My routine had become one of waking with anxiety in my gut and tears in my eyes. My body ached from the heaviness of nightly spiritual battles, crying out to God to save me. My husband, my earthly anchor, had strayed from our marriage to another woman. The marriage that once felt like it held me steady and kept hope alive for me, was now facing a pain that left me in darkness and feeling hopeless to survive the storm. The vessel of my life was being wrecked. Faith, as I understood it, began to feel distant and unknown.

I found myself in a strange place of longing to be anchored by an adamant faith that God would rescue me from all my pain, yet despising what felt like the most cliché Christian "pat answer" scriptures ever over-spoken. They would show up daily in my text messages, inbox, and daily conversations.

"Hope is an anchor for your soul, Rhiannon," they would say.

"Can I throat-punch you?" would be what every fiber of my being would want to say in return. I felt as though that anchor of hope was for someone else, while for me it was actually hopeless.

Months into this terrible storm, I traveled with my oldest daughter to New York, where she was recording her first album. As I sat in the back of the studio listening to her hauntingly beautiful voice sing songs of worship, God led me to the peculiar story of Paul's shipwreck in Acts 27. The passage described the terrible storm that Paul and his shipmates experienced as *"having blotted out the sun and the stars"* (27:20). That's where I felt I was: Every hope of light blotted out against my will, immersed in a terrible, uncontrollable, dark storm. Having a faith in hope felt like an anchor, all right, but one that weighed me down instead of holding me steady.

The description of the storm Paul experienced resonated perfectly with the despair I felt. But then came verse 22: *"But take courage! None of you will lose your lives, even though the ship will go down."* As I read the verse, God gently whispered to my weary soul, "You will be wrecked, but you will be saved." In those whispered words, a hope like one I had never understood before awoke in me. A hope that, if I could cling to tightly and not relinquish my position to the enemy, would rescue me. I embraced the wreckage—the beautiful, messy wreckage—and found my true anchor. The nature of human sin and this fallen world blindsided my life like I never imagined it could, but an adamant faith was being formed in me by being completely wrecked and wholly saved.

It's unfortunate, but I have found it to be true, that in one way or another everyone in this world will face storms during which they may feel as if all light is blotted out and loss is imminent. Wreckage will happen. Yet, we have a Heavenly Father who is our anchor in the storm. He tells us, "Take courage in your hold to Me. You will wreck, but I am with you. Hold on and I will save you." The anchor isn't an object that weighs us down; it is a Heavenly Father who holds us steady. Being anchored in adamant faith isn't about a false safety that says "you'll be okay." It's about allowing yourself to say, "I'm not okay. I am being wrecked, but the One that is hope in the wreckage will save me."

Reflect and Respond

Is there an area of your life in which you have been holding the pieces of wreckage as a weighted anchor? If so, how can you choose to hold on to the true anchor of God?

_____

_____

_____

Is there an area of wreckage in your life now that you can begin to lean in to an adamant faith that God will save you?

_____

_____

_____

Rhiannon Rutledge and her husband of 21 years are committed to sharing their wreckage story with the hope of demonstrating God's restoring power in lives and marriages. Along with three amazing kids, Rhiannon has learned to embrace who God has made her to be: a woman desperate for God, a wife who loves to write, and a stay-at-home mom who adores a great shade of lipstick.

Day 9

Adamant Faith is Anchored in

God's Faithfulness

PATSY PEARSON

For the Lord is good and his love endures forever;
his faithfulness continues through all generations.

Psalm 100:5 (NIV)

I can still see my mom with the memory of my heart: deep dimples in her smile, which appeared so readily. My mom was my hero, and my best example of faith in action.

As a little girl, she felt called to the mission field, and had a vision of ministering to people in a distant part of the world. She went to a Bible college to prepare to follow God's plan for her life. While she was there, she became aware of a certain handsome classmate, but because of the strict rules of the college, they were not allowed to date until the last few weeks of their senior year. The man who would become my dad was also very aware of this sweet young lady, and hastened to ask her out as soon as it was okay. He was also called into the ministry and spent a year doing evangelistic work before they married.

Together, they spent about ten years in evangelistic work and in pastorates. By the time they left for the mission field of Indonesia in 1946, they had three daughters in tow.

Mom faced many challenges as a missionary wife in Indonesia as she and Dad raised four daughters in an environment that presented many challenges. I can remember a trip of two or three days when my older sister and I accompanied them in a motorboat down a muddy brown river populated by crocodiles. We went to a village where the sight of white people was rare, and brought the gospel to those people. Looking back, I think of the fears that could have come to her riding through crocodile-filled waters with two young daughters. My younger sister was only a toddler, so she had been left in the care of a woman back at their mission base. How would I have felt, leaving my youngest behind while exposing my two older daughters to the dangers of this trip?

Yet I never saw a sign of fear or uncertainty in Mom. She had faith that the one who had called her into his service would care for her loved ones. She lived a life of adamant faith through the circumstances they faced on the mission field. She loved the people they served, and it showed.

Later on, when my Dad experienced a heart attack and stroke, her faith in God's ability to give her strength was outstanding. I watched her keep a steady confidence that God would heal him, and if not, that he would continue to hold them both in his hands. She always had a positive attitude and believed God would see them through every challenge they faced.

My mother faced misunderstandings with friends, discouragements in ministry, and many health concerns for Dad and herself, yet her faith in God's provision was unwavering.

In the Bible, God gave many promises to his people, but often those promises were conditional on their response. "If you . . . then I will" is the phrase that echoes through much of his communication to his people. When we are faithful to him, he shows his faithfulness to us. The more we fill our thoughts and minds with God's word, the more we give our faith a chance to grow.

Sometimes you may not receive the things you want as soon as you want them, but he is trustworthy and will answer his faithful ones in his perfect time.

Hebrews 11:13 tells us something about those who were living by faith: *"All these people were still living by faith when they died. They did not receive the things promised; they only saw them and welcomed them from a distance, admitting that they were foreigners and strangers on earth."*

As I look back on the things I learned from watching Mom on the mission field, I saw an unshakeable faith in God's ability to help in any situation. I learned an attitude of gratitude from her that has made a huge difference in my own life when encountering difficult times. Her adamant faith has inspired me to continue to trust God through the journey he has given me.

Reflect and Respond

Have you found God to be faithful to you? Why or why not?

_____

_____

_____

On what do you base your belief in God's faithfulness?

_____

_____

_____

Patsy Pearson is a mother and grandmother who lives in New Hope, Minnesota. She loves going to her grandkids' basketball games, volunteering, writing, and good coffee.

Day 10

Adamant Faith is Anchored in

His Symphony

ASHLEY MCKEOWN

Even in the madness, there is peace, drowning out the voices all around me. Through all of this chaos, you are writing a symphony.

Switch (feat. Dillon Chase). Lyrics to "Symphony." Symphony EP, 2019

I was angry at God.

How could he let me feel this lost and broken? How could he allow me to endure more pain than I'd ever known?

I laid in my bed at 3 a.m. in the darkness weeping, silently crying out to God, begging him for help. I didn't want to end my life, but I couldn't live this way anymore.

My postpartum depression had reached its peak. I had thought that things were supposed to be better now that my daughter was out of the newborn phase. She was supposed to cry less, I was supposed to sleep more, and maybe we'd finally start to bond.

But my daughter's hip surgery at 4 months old took us to a new low. My depression skyrocketed as my baby cried constantly, never slept, and demanded my comfort at all hours.

We had no idea at the time, but I would later be diagnosed with sleep apnea, and the insane sleep deprivation I was experiencing was affecting my depression so much that I experienced a state of psychosis.

I lost touch with reality and myself, spiraling downward until the night I thought of ending it all.

"God, why have you forsaken me?" I silently pleaded through the darkness.

I didn't hear God that night, but I knew he was there. I knew that he wanted me to draw closer to him because he was going to work this for his good. He was orchestrating something bigger than my pain.

And as much as I hated what I was going through, I knew he would keep his promise.

"For I know the plans I have for you," declares the LORD, "plans to prosper you and not to harm you, plans to give you hope and a future" (Jeremiah 29:11, NIV).

I've leaned on this verse my entire life, and I've seen God time and time again prove his love for me. I knew he had a future for me. I knew that my faith needed to be stronger than my anger.

The morning after my breakdown, I started being more honest about what I was really experiencing. My husband went along with me to my therapy appointment, and the three of us talked through treatment options and an action plan in case things ever got that bad again. Healing was slow, and each step forward took strength and faith.

Postpartum depression nearly destroyed me. I'd always been someone who didn't know their purpose in life, but after I gave birth, I lost all sense of self. Healing meant not just treating my depression, but also finding my identity.

Through that refining process, God used my pain for his glory, allowing it to completely transform me. I'm not the same person I was before I gave birth.

And though it's been two-and-a-half years, recovery has been slow. I didn't heal overnight.

Once I began to be honest with others about my journey, other women reached out to share their own similar experiences. My story has given me a way to connect with others who feel lost and broken. I started blogging. I created a Facebook group for moms. I help with my church's women's ministry and speak at mental health conventions. I get to reach out and hug moms who've been through things far worse than I because my story has given them the confidence to vocalize their own struggles.

And all of that is possible because God has a plan for me. God knows my future, and all I have to do is keep believing that the symphony he has composed is more beautiful than any suffering I may experience.

Reflect and Respond

Have you ever found yourself drowning in the chaos around you? Where do you turn when things seem to be falling apart?

_____

_____

_____

Do you believe God is writing your beautiful symphony? How can you trust in him to sustain you through the highs and lows of life?

_____

_____

_____

Ashley McKeown blogs about imperfect motherhood and mental health. Her blog, _Everybody's Fed, Nobody's Dead_, reaches moms worldwide through her honesty and humor. When not furiously typing, she is often found at Chick-Fil-A, binge-watching _Gilmore Girls_, or bribing her toddler with suckers. Ashley resides in Minnesota with her husband and daughter.

Day 11

Adamant Faith is Anchored in

Remembering Who God Is

RACHEL ROEN

Who is like you, Lord God Almighty?
You, Lord, are mighty, and your faithfulness surrounds you.

Psalm 89:8 (NIV)

I once worked for a company based out of California that no one I knew had ever heard of, and several people questioned their legitimacy and my safety in working for them. As part of my job, I was required to fly out to California and be picked up by what they described over the phone as a "creepy white van," a van with the windows blacked out. But by the time I received that phone call, I had already purchased my ticket and was leaving in the next day or two.

Telling people that a creepy white van is picking them up may have not been the company's best idea. Up until then, I was fairly sure about the job. I had experienced the usual nerves that come from trying something new, but overall I felt like it was where God was leading me. I had looked up the company online, and it sounded like a legitimate company. However, I did wonder what on earth I was getting into after that phone call.

It turns out that I did, in fact, get picked up by the creepy white van. But the reason it had blacked-out windows was so that people couldn't see the equipment in the back of the van. The job was to set up equipment and show company-made videos for school assembly programs. After training in

California, I was paired with another female coworker. We lived on the road for several months. After Christmas break, we switched and worked with someone else. It was a hard job at times—I got tired of living out of a suitcase, eating fast food, being on the road almost continually, and working out differences with my coworker without having outside friends and interests to help ease the situation—but it also gave me the opportunity to see different states. Despite my initial reservations and the creepy white van that picked me up on my first day, God was with me throughout the two years that I worked that job, leading me on despite the questions others had.

Adamant faith is trusting in a faithful God. Often I feel like I need to do something or get it right. The reality is that it's not about what I do; it's simply remembering what God has done and knowing and believing that he will continue to work.

God is faithful even when I am not. Recently I was facing a situation that caused uncertainty and anxiety. During that time, I felt like God was reminding me that he was still in control.

In Joshua 4:1–3, God commands Joshua to have the Israelites take stones to place by the Jordan River that they had miraculously crossed over. They were to use these as a remembrance of God's faithfulness. This pile of 12 stones (one for each tribe) was to remind them. Clearly, remembering is important to God. Our adamant faith comes from remembering God's faithfulness. Over the last several weeks God has been reminding me of how he has been at work in my life.

He reminded me that he has taken care of little details—things as small as schedule conflicts with a job. Things that might not seem all that significant, yet show he cares about my life.

He reminded me that he placed me in environments where I can learn about him.

He reminded me of how he has spoken to me on a walk or in a quiet place.

He reminded me that he was close by and comforted me when my aunt died of cancer.

He reminded that he gave me hope when I didn't have any.

Each of these memories is like an Israelite stone that I can hang onto when life gets hard again. Each one is a stone to place to build the "monument" of how God is faithful.

I don't know what my future holds, but I know that God cares and is with me. I simply have to believe that God is with me and will keep his promises. In Matthew 28:20, Jesus promises to be with us always. In Joshua 1:5, God promises Joshua that he will never leave or forsake him. Deuteronomy 31:6 also mentions God never leaving. Hebrews 13:5 quotes these passages and applies them to us as Christians.

God has been with me, and because he has been faithful in the past, I can trust him for the future. Having adamant faith is believing that God is faithful and remembering all that he has done.

Reflect and Respond

Look back and find God's faithfulness in your life. What memories can you use as stone reminders of his faithfulness no matter what you are facing today?

_____

_____

_____

Rachel Roen enjoys learning, traveling, and spending time with friends. She recently completed her master's degree in strategic leadership and is looking forward to the next adventure God has in store.

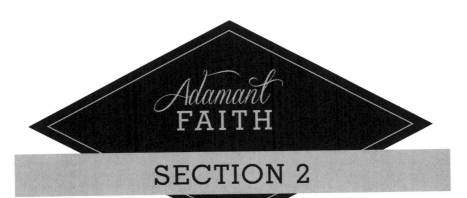

SECTION 2

Adamant Faith is
Greater than...

Day 12

Adamant Faith is Greater than

Stress

KELLY RADI

Are you tired? Worn out? Burned out? Come to me.
Get away with me and you'll recover your life.
I'll show you how to take a real rest.
Walk with me and work with me—watch how I do it.
Learn the unforced rhythms of grace.
I won't lay anything heavy or ill-fitting on you.
Keep company with me and you'll learn to live freely and lightly.

Matthew 11:28–30 (MSG)

I lowered myself into the bubble-filled tub and took a sip of herbal tea. It was ten at night and, after multiple trips to the bathroom and several bedtime stories, kisses, and hugs, I'd finally gotten the girls to sleep. The flickering light from the candle I'd lit to help me relax bounced off the mirror, reminding me that I still needed to clean the bathroom. My husband was gone for the fourth night that week, and I was exhausted. I woke up an hour later, shivering in a tepid bath with fingers wrinkled like raisins.

I was an at-home mom who felt like I had no time for myself and never enough time to do all the things I should be doing. I'd slip my version of self-care in wherever I could. It might mean a late-night bubble bath or plopping the kids in the stroller for a power walk. I read the magazines and bought into the commercialized concept of self-care, yet I never quite felt rested or refreshed.

Get a massage. Drink a green smoothie. Slip into a bubble bath. Light a scented candle. Take a walk. Smear on a mud mask.

Spend just two minutes on Pinterest or Instagram and you'll find the latest self-care must-dos being thrust into your already over-abundant to-do lists. I don't know about you, but sometimes this self-care stuff just seems like one more thing I *should* be doing.

Some days, practicing self-care seems more like a distraction than a solution. When it adds stress, is it actually self-care?

Have we turned life's little luxuries into Band-Aid fixes for ongoing problems? Have we replaced prayer with protein powder? Smoothies and power walks are good things—great things, actually—but they will not fix your overbooked calendar, your overstuffed inbox, and your overstressed life.

Don't get me wrong. I believe in taking care of oneself. I enjoy immersing myself in a good book. I'll take any excuse I can to schedule a massage. And I can indulge in a caramel macchiato with extra whip like it's nobody's business. But, in reality, self-care is not always so sexy. It may include ratty sweatpants and a seven-year-old sports bra for a before-the-roosters-crow fitness class. It may mean sticking to a strict budget to reduce that pile of ugly debt you accrued in college. It may mean saying no to a toxic relationship or another volunteer commitment, and yes to spending more time at home.

It definitely means getting real and honest with yourself—and getting down on your knees before God, which is exactly what I did following my aha moment in the bathtub.

While that massage may feel good and help you relax at the time, you might want to ask yourself, "Is this a temporary fix to a larger problem?"

That larger problem is the s-word. Stress. What are you doing to help reduce your stress? Are you addressing it, or are you hiding it under a blanket of self-care rituals? Are you asking God to help you adjust your lifestyle so you're not constantly exhausted and too anxious to function? Are you praying over your self-imposed expectations so you don't feel the need to escape by diving headfirst into a lavender-scented bubble bath?

Is it possible your "need" to practice today's self-care trends might be because you're actually disconnected from Jesus and his idea of real self-care—making intentional choices that prioritize your faith and your long-term, overall wellbeing?

Jesus is the ultimate stress reducer!

Imagine life with less anxiety and fewer feelings of inadequacy, where mud masks and yoga are ways to celebrate your life, not escape from it. Where joy and peace are the norm, not an elusive goal.

How can you achieve that life you long for? Start really caring for you—*all* of you.

- Forget what looks good to others and do what *is* good for you.

- Spend less time on social media comparing your life to others and more time creating the life he wants for you.

- Surround yourself with a tribe of supporters—your spirit sisters—who fill your tank with goodness, kindness, and honesty. Be the friend you'd like to have.

- Look at your schedule and self-imposed expectations with a realistic eye. Seriously, there's no way to squeeze twenty hours of work into an eight-hour work day.

- Be adamant in your faith. Trust that God has a beautiful plan for you— one that is abundant in hope and overflowing with opportunities.

As Matthew 6:33 (NIV) explains, *"Seek first his kingdom and his righteousness, and all these things will be given to you as well."*

Yes, you have many responsibilities and people depending on you. But you can't take care of others if you are depleted yourself. So, please, my friends, start with you. Enjoy your baths and barre classes. Breathe in your essential oil-diffused air. But also choose to drink in his presence. Feed on his word. Be intentional with your time and energy. Spend time in self-reflection, scripture, and prayer!

You are worthy of real self-care.

Reflect and Respond

What obstacles are getting in the way of your real self-care? What can you say "no" to today that will give you margin and reduce your stress?

_____

_____

_____

What is your favorite self-care ritual? How can you incorporate it into your schedule so it becomes a way to celebrate the joy and peace you feel as a woman of adamant faith?

_____

_____

_____

Kelly Radi is a sought-after motivational speaker and award-winning author of *Wonder-Full: Activate Your Inner Superpowers (No Cape Required)*. Authentic and relatable, Kelly equips and empowers women to find—and use—their unique, God-given superpowers to live Wonder-Full lives. Connect with Kelly at www.raditowrite.com.

Day 13

Adamant Faith is Greater than

Meaningless Signs

EMILY E. RYAN

Then Jesus told him, "Because you have seen me, you have believed; blessed are those who have not seen and yet have believed."

John 20:29 (NIV)

A high fever, coupled with a glassy-eyed stare from a child who is too young to communicate, is a combination of symptoms no parent ever wants to encounter. So when my two-year-old son Canaan transformed from a bouncing, bubbly toddler into a lethargic, unresponsive little boy in a matter of an hour, my husband and I made a frantic trip to the emergency room for some answers. After several tests, blood work, x-rays, and IV drips, Canaan remained unchanged and we were no closer to figuring out the source of his condition than when we arrived.

Several hours later, at three o'clock in the morning, I found myself strapped to a hospital gurney with Canaan in my arms as we were wheeled into the back of an ambulance. He was being transferred to Texas Children's Hospital, where they hoped the pediatric unit would be able to provide more answers.

As I felt the heat radiating from his little body, I tried desperately to keep every worst-case scenario from playing out in my mind. I prayed that God would heal him. I prayed for answers. And I prayed for some sign that all of my desperate pleas were being heard.

I knew we would be traveling north on the freeway and—depending on my position in the ambulance and the angle of the windows—there was a good chance I'd be able to see my church's 170-foot tall cross spotlighted in the darkness. Oh, how I wanted to see that cross! I watched familiar landmarks fly by the windows and craned my neck for just a glimpse of the cross when I could tell we were close. But I never saw it.

At first, I was devastated. All I wanted was a simple "sign" that God was listening, but instead I got nothing. I felt lost, alone, forgotten, and scared. If I couldn't "see" God, then surely he couldn't see me.

But almost as soon as the thought formulated in my mind, the truth of God's Word swept in and set me straight. I didn't need to see a cross to know that God was listening. I also didn't need to "feel" his presence to know that he had never left my side. I understood then that faith is understanding that the reality of who God is does not depend upon my perception of him, that adamant faith is greater than any meaningless sign.

I never did get a sign that my little boy would be alright. Instead, we left the hospital 24 hours later with a perfectly healthy child and no answers as to why he had been so sick. But I had learned that the absence of a sign from God does not equate to the absence of God.

Have you ever prayed for a sign? Almost all of us have. Sometimes we receive the signs we ask for, like Gideon did in Judges 6, or like the sign of the rainbow in Genesis 9. But other times God invites us to simply trust and believe, even when our eyes cannot see him, our ears do not hear him, and our fingers cannot reach out and feel the evidence of his goodness.

Because we all experience times when God feels invisible or apathetic to us, we must prepare in advance by strengthening our faith through his Word. How well do you really know what the Bible says about your God? Immerse yourself now in his truths so that the next time God seems invisible to you, the truths you have burned into memory will eclipse any doubts you may have. Although you may still find yourself praying for a "sign," don't be surprised when that sign is simply his Word manifesting itself clearly and lovingly into your heart.

Reflect and Respond

When have you prayed that God would show you a sign instead of relying on faith?

_____

_____

_____

What sign did Thomas ask for John 20:24–29? How will you use Jesus's response to Thomas to strengthen your own faith?

_____

_____

_____

Emily E. Ryan is a minister's wife, mother of four, and junior high English teacher. She is a frequent speaker and the author of several books including _Guilt-Free Quiet Times_ and _Who Has Your Heart? The Single Woman's Pursuit of Godliness_. Connect with her at www.emilyeryan.com.

Day 14

Adamant Faith is Greater than

Staying in Bed

ELIZABETH LINDBERG RAYFORD

Why are you cast down, O my soul,
and why are you in turmoil within me?
Hope in God; for I shall again praise him,
my salvation and my God.

Psalm 42:5 (ESV)

The wind whistled against the east bedroom window above my head. The louder it howled, the further I sank into the warmth of my bed. Curled onto my left side, Billy snored peacefully, his three-year-old body heat drawing me to be still. To my right, my phone lit up the dark and bellowed, "Get up. Get. Up. It's time. Right. now. Get up." I hit snooze, and the room was once again calm.

Sometimes life feels too heavy, and comforters too cozy, and the bed beckons, *Stay with me just a little longer.*

Soon enough, the sweet three-year old awoke. When he wouldn't be kept down, I realized that I needed to get up too. But something held me there. It wasn't just tiredness. I could have stayed in bed all day. I mean, not *really*—my child demanded breakfast. But I definitely wanted to stay. And I don't think I'm uncommon at all in that dream of the perfect day. In fact, I know I'm not, because I recently polled a room full of mothers and the common denominator in every single day dream included napping. I don't know any parents who wouldn't claim sleep deprivation, at least for their children's littlest years.

But, there was something else holding me to the bed that morning. A myriad of metaphors come to mind, but the reality of it was just very simply *grief.*

Whether it's new, in the days immediately following a loss, or years after the initial event—as it was for me on this particular day—grief drops a certain heaviness. It had been more than three years since my husband died, yet that heaviness is hard to shake and it can feel debilitating. And on my own, it's not something I can lift.

David wrote about this in Psalm 42. Though he wanted more than anything for his heart to soar and his tongue to sing in unbridled praise, he felt stuck in the depths. In verse 5 he says, *"Why are you cast down, O my soul, and why are you in turmoil within me?"* Yet instead of staying in that place in his mind, David continues, *"Hope in God; for I will again praise Him; my salvation and my God."*

David took a step of faith, believing that God would restore his soul to a posture of praise. With adamant faith, David actively remembered God's strength and fulfilled promises. Though his soul was tired and though he did not feel like praising God, he got out of bed anyway.

I love this lament because it's evidence that, while David moved forward in faith, he didn't ignore what he was feeling. His soul was tired, and it had solid reason to be. He was opposed on all sides and in such great pain that he said, *"My tears have been my food day and night."*

Moving forward does not mean letting go or moving on. It means feeling the hurt, letting it matter, and bringing it with you into each next step in faith.

But faith is powerless unless the object of that faith is great—which is why it is so important that David remembered God's faithfulness. It's not the remembering that allowed him to move forward, but *what* and *who* he was remembering.

When we have adamant faith, we're not simply believing something for the sake of agreement, but rather we are placing our trust intentionally on someone who has been proven greater than our circumstances. Even on the days when our metaphorical and literal bodies drag, God shows up and we move forward together.

So I got up that morning, and many mornings like it. I made breakfast. I laughed and cried with my kids. We watched some tv when my body dragged and played hide-and-seek when I got a second wind. And most of all, we thanked God for the present blessings.

I showed up. Ripping myself from the bed has been no easy task on grief days, and sometimes I move through the hours just one step at a time. Yet, on those days I focus on remembering God's strength and fulfilled promises to restore hope and praise to my soul.

Stepping into adamant faith leads me to move forward in his strength so I can show up for my kids, my loved ones, my roles, myself, and God's bright plans for the future.

Reflect and Respond

Is there a specific season or time in your life during which it was particularly difficult to get out of bed?

_____

_____

_____

What role has faith played in your ability to show up for your life?

_____

_____

_____

Elizabeth Lindberg Rayford was born and raised a Minnesota girl. She currently lives in Winona and gets to love two imaginative boys with her brand new husband, Davin. Elizabeth delights in changing seasons, vanilla lattes, hand lettering, and dinosaur noises. She writes about motherhood, grief, and God's faithfulness at lizziejlindberg. com.

Day 15

Adamant Faith is Greater than

Life's Uncertainties

JACLYN LOWEEN

All these people were still living by faith when they died.
They did not receive the things promised; they only saw them and welcomed them
from a distance, admitting that they were foreigners and strangers on earth.

Hebrews 11:13 (NIV)

Is there a place or time in your past that—if given the opportunity—you would return to relive?

For me, that place is South Korea. And maybe it's not so much the place, but the time of life and the people I met that I would return to if I could.

I moved away from the United States at the age of 22—one year into my marriage, inexperienced in my career and missions. I was young, excited for the adventure, and enthusiastic in embracing the unknown. My mind and heart were fueled with the powerful contradictions of a young heart full of faith—naiveté and confidence, carefreeness and certainty, simplicity and vision.

Seven years later, I returned a very different woman. This became evident one day when a friend who knew me well and whom I trusted deeply came for a visit. In the midst of our conversation, she asked how I was doing with the transition and with God. Before I even had time to edit my words, I said, "I still believe in God. I just can't say that I like him right now."

That stopped the conversation. And even as I tried to laugh it off, I knew deep down my faith was faltering. I felt so lost in every area of my life that my mouth had inadvertently confessed how deep my struggle went.

I felt like I didn't fit into the conversations other women were having about the "best" diapers, car seats, and strollers to purchase. While away, I had figured out how to make do with what limited options I had. What should have been a normal weekly activity—going to Walmart for groceries—overwhelmed me. There were too many options, too many decisions, and too many numbers to calculate. I could find anything I wanted but instead of feeling comforting, it felt daunting. It was just one more reminder that I didn't fit in the place I used to call home.

I had gained a wealth of knowledge about myself, others, and culture because of my foreign setting and teaching experiences. And though such learning was good and necessary, it all but ruined me at re-entry. The way I had learned to approach life abroad didn't fit once we moved back to the U.S., taking a bit of the confidence out of my sails, harnessing the carefreeness of my youth, and eroding the simplicity of my earlier visions. Maturity often seems to come at the cost of childlike faith.

When my husband and I left, it was just the two of us on an adventure to see what God could do with us. When we returned as a family of four with one more on the way, I was not sure I even knew the person who had left all those years before. I couldn't remember much about her or how she viewed the world, God, and the future. Try as I might, I couldn't restore the childlike faith that made her so brave when the adventure of leaving was reversed and we returned home.

Seven years have passed since our return to state-side soil. We are now a family of six, and I have changed jobs four times. I have learned more than I ever wanted to know about transitions, trusting God's plans, and adapting to his purposes no matter one's location or vocation. I have come to rest in the reality that God's always going to make old things new because he is creative, faithful, and good. And not just in the general sense; he is good to me. I can trust his faithfulness even when I feel my faith is wavering or absent.

But looking forward and believing God is good takes mental, physical, emotional, and spiritual fortitude. Some days I catch myself looking in the rearview mirror of my life, feeling a bit of that loss again—wishing that I could return to our first place, our first people, our first mission. Cognitively, I *know* that even if my feet returned, I would not find what I am looking for in that mirror.

Remembering the relationships, adventure, and simplicity of a time long gone can rob me of my joy or it can help me refocus on God's faithfulness. But in order for that to happen, I have to do the hard work of letting myself grieve the blessings of the past, recall the blessing of transitions, continue on to praising God for present blessings, and land at a childlike faith that helps me believe the best blessings are yet to come.

Just as the men and women described in Hebrews 11 lived their entire lives based on faith in what was yet to come, I am called and equipped to do the same: To let faith be my guide more often than my rearview mirror. To let faith focus my eyes forward. To believe, just as the Hebrews declared, that I am a stranger here but am still able to live faithfully because of what is coming, even if I die waiting to see the fruition of the promises my faith is built upon.

Maybe you, too, are fighting to return to a childlike faith. Maybe—like me— you are on a journey toward understanding and processing everything that God's plans have led you to and from. Can I encourage you to begin recording your memories and progress along the way?

There is nothing that heals quite like setting words to experiences and allowing God to work through your fingertips to teach you about who he is, who you are, and how the moments of your life are building you up to greater purposes because he has good plans for you. I pray you can create space in your life to allow God to bring back those memories you need to recall in order to live well—by faith—the part of the journey you are on right now.

Reflect and Respond

Circumstances and transitions in our life can sometimes cause us to falter in our faith in God's promises to us. How have the transitions in your life both shaken you up and strengthened your trust in God?

_____

_____

_____

How can you choose to muster the courage to ask God to give you back the childlike faith of your younger years? In what ways can you begin taking steps toward attaining it?

_____

_____

_____

Jaclyn Loween is a wife, mother, and teacher who is passionate about community living, learning, writing, running, and inviting people to her table. It is her hope that her words of remembrance and reflection record a story of God's faithfulness that will be passed to future generations. Find more inspiration, instruction, and encouragement at jaclynloween.com.

Day 16

Adamant Faith is Greater than

Brokenness

ANGIE HERDER

And my God will meet all your needs
according to the riches of his glory in Christ Jesus.
Philippians 4:19 (NIV)

The wedding was a dream. My mom made my dress, we danced and celebrated with family until just before dawn, and I married a man I truly loved—my first boyfriend.

Yet, just seven years later, I found myself in the midst of a painful divorce.

I never imagined when I walked down that aisle to marry my husband that we would go through a divorce. It just wasn't in the plan. But there I was. My put-together life crumbled before my eyes and dropped me to my knees. I was completely broken and, on top of that, I was broke. I was a stay-at-home mom for a couple years prior to the divorce and then started a part-time job at a fitness center, hoping and praying it would become full-time.

I wanted to prove to myself that I could make it on my own, but a fair amount of pride and a stubborn Italian streak also kept me from moving back home with my parents. Because my name was still on the house with my ex-husband, I couldn't get approved for another credit card. The only one I had was from Menards, so that's where I bought groceries for myself and my two children.

I fed them first. I ate last. I paid the bills with the largest late fees first and then paid the other bills as I had the money. I eventually hit a new low and called my mom to ask for money. I never imagined I would need to do that at almost 30 years old. But my parents came through and bailed me out. It was so humbling.

Many times, I would allow my children to watch never-ending hours of television. Before the divorce, I took them to the park and went for walks or bike rides with them, but now I barely had the energy to get through the day. Instead of continuing to make homemade meals, I switched to processed meals out of a box.

I remember Mom telling me it was a win if I fed my kids and had them bathed.

I was so broke I was at the point that my stomach turned every time money was brought up. I winced every time I checked my bank account.

I was broken, the loneliness and hurt in my heart so overwhelming that I knew some massive healing needed to take place.

But it never once crossed my mind that I was poor. To me, being poor would mean I didn't have anything. And I knew without a doubt my God was there for me.

The whole time that I was struggling to make a new life for my kids and me, I also knew I was wrapped in the embrace of my Lord and Savior. He was working in me—in that broke and broken place. He was building my character and growing me into a better mom, preparing me for my future career as a personal trainer and nutritionist. Those areas in which I struggled so deeply after the divorce became the tools God now uses through me to help others.

God gave me a new dream: to live independently and support my kids after the divorce. We may have been broke for a time, but we always had Jesus.

And when we have him, we're never poor.

Reflect and Respond

When has God used a tough time in your life to grow you into a better version of yourself?

_____

_____

_____

Consider whether you truly trust God to meet your needs. In what areas of your life is that most difficult?

_____

_____

_____

After being a single mom for six years, **Angie Herder** has remarried and, together with her new husband, has formed her own version of a "Brady Brunch" family. She devotes her time and energy to her family and her personal training and nutrition clients. It's Angie's mission to point all who cross her path to Jesus.

Day 17

Adamant Faith is Greater than

My Reality

KRISTEN OSTREM

*...He will achieve infinitely more than your greatest request,
your most unbelievable dream,
and exceed your wildest imagination!*

Ephesians 3:20 (The Passion)

"When is this season going to change?" I cried out, annoyed, as I drove home one evening.

Some days, I enjoy singleness and have patience for this stage. On other days, as a single and ready-to-*be-done*-mingling Millennial who is edging closer to 30, I can find myself frustrated with people, timing, and reality.

Amidst lonely days and familiar rhythms of life, my soul awaits something new—the next phase of my story to begin. I look forward to cooking meals for more than one person, driving home with someone else after family gatherings, and having a man with whom I can share life's moments.

While singleness is my current status, the desire for marriage is often on the forefront of my mind.

I have prayed for my husband. I have been on multiple dates throughout my twenties. I have written many journal entries. I have paid for subscriptions and dated online. I have made my "list" of hoped-for qualities in a spouse, and I also have condensed lists. I have gleaned relationship insights from preachers and authors. I have engaged in different young adult communities.

If thinking and conversing about a particular topic was enough to earn someone a college degree, by now, I should have a PhD in assessing the plight of dating in today's world—or at least in my journey through it all.

Last January, as I was processing the dreaded moment of telling a guy friend that I didn't see our relationship going further, an older female friend approached me during a worship service with a word she believed God wanted to speak to me. She said, "I feel like God wants to [ask you], 'Do you trust me?'"

Her question helped me say no to this guy friend, but I pondered its meaning on and off throughout the rest of the year. "Do I trust you, God? Do I trust you for what?" I wondered.

This year, I asked God for a keyword, verse, or theme for me to focus on. He highlighted Psalm 46:10: *"Be still and know that I am God..."* In another translation, the verse reads to *"Cease striving and know..."*

As an achievement-driven individual, when I have particular goals in mind, I am motivated to work toward making them happen. However, it can also be easy to see the chasm between a future dream and my present reality and feel that I haven't done *enough* to close the gap.

Thoughts of, "I shouldn't have done *that*," or "if I do *this*, maybe I would be further along" come to mind. Regarding relationships, maybe if I post more on social media, then the guy I like will see me. On the other hand, if my hashtag choices aren't perfect, he might be turned off to the idea.

Really?

If I conclude my worthiness or destiny hinges on something as minuscule as my use of an Instagram hashtag, then my heart needs examining!

Ultimately, I desire for God to get the glory in and through my life. Yet, based on my current belief system, if my dream does or doesn't happen, whose fault is the failure or success?

Pride would say of successes, "I did that," while shame would say of failures, "I didn't do enough." Yet, God reminds us—as he did in Psalm 46:10—to place our faith in him alone. He invites us to daily give up control and adamantly trust his voice to lead us, because his ways are perfect.

The Lord is faithful and will complete what he started in us. He knows the full picture and is more than capable to do whatever he wants, whenever he wants.

In fact, Ephesians 3:20 tells us that God is at work to achieve more than our greatest request, most unbelievable dream, or wildest imagination! I have seen this verse in action throughout my current season, as God exposes fears and wrong beliefs to heal and set me free with truth.

There is nothing that compares to his presence and goodness, and whether or not any of my future plans come to be, I want God to work Ephesians 3:20 in my life more than anything! May he lead our steps, may our faith be unswayed by circumstances, and may he be glorified as we trust him fully and watch for his wonders to unfold.

Reflect and Respond

What things are you waiting, hoping, or praying for?

_____

_____

_____

In what ways is God asking you to trust him?

_____

_____

_____

What wrong beliefs or insecurities might he be asking you to exchange for his wonderful Truth?

_____

_____

_____

Kristen Ostrem loves being a daughter, sister, and aunt and living the adventurous life Jesus offers. Along with the excitement of free opportunities, worship concerts, and hard-scoop ice cream, she has a heart for the Church and enjoys traveling, playing music, and writing.

Day 18

Adamant Faith is Greater than
My Storm

NANCY HOLTE

For I know the one in whom I trust and I am sure that he is able
to guard what I have entrusted to him until the day of his return.

2 Timothy 1:12b (NLT)

It all started with a tornado.

While my husband and I were serving on a mission trip in Europe, four tornadoes touched down in our little town, leaving a mess that can't adequately be described. When we arrived home, the town looked like a war zone. The damage at our house was minimal, but there was damage. Because the tornado hit in late September, and so many homes were hit, the cleanup and repairs would stretch far into the following spring.

A month later we found out that the cancer my husband had been diagnosed with five years ago was no longer in remission. Multiple Myeloma is a treatable cancer, not a curable cancer, so this wasn't unexpected but definitely not what we were hoping for. He started a new type of chemotherapy, and thankfully didn't have any adverse reactions, so other than missing a half-day of work every week it felt like no big deal. When this type of cancer raises its ugly head, it just needs to be knocked back down like you do in a game of Whac-A-Mole . . . except this isn't a game.

A few months later, at his quarterly checkup, we found out that the chemo hadn't really done the job it was supposed to and there was a lesion growing on the bone in his arm. So, after what felt like a thousand more tests, he moved on to radiation therapy.

Just when I thought the tornadoes and radiation had given us enough troubles to deal with my 92-year-old mother got sick. She lives 1500 miles away and needed me to fly out to help her twice in the same month. That's when I started to feel like I was right in the middle of my own personal tornado.

You know that feeling when you want to be in two places at once? That's how I felt. My husband was starting radiation therapy, and I was leaving to be with my mom who needed me even more than my husband did. And tornado-related calls from the insurance company seemed to be coming in on a regular basis.

Everything came to a head when I was trying to get to my grandson's last preschool program of the year. The plane to my mom's was leaving late in the day so I would still have time to go to his program before heading to the airport. I left home in plenty of time, but due to a series of unfortunate events, I ended up running late.

I would have been devastated to miss my grandson's program but arriving on time was definitely going to be a challenge. I knew my grandson's program was about to start and I was still a few blocks away. I managed to miss every single stoplight on the way to his school!

That's when I started banging my head on the steering wheel and remembered a line from the movie, *Return to Me*, "Why does God hate me?" At the very moment the words escaped my mouth, I stopped myself. Because, though I found the line funny in the movie, it is so far from the truth that I felt convicted about even saying it out loud.

God does not hate me; I know that beyond a shadow of a doubt. And even though my world seems to be spinning out of control, my adamant faith reminds me that it's not. God has a plan, and because I am sure of his love, I can be equally sure that it'll all work together for my good and his glory. He is trustworthy and faithful.

I'd love to tie this all neatly together and tell you that everything did indeed work out for good but, as I write this, I'm still in the middle of the storm. Though my husband is done with his radiation, we don't know if it worked or when we'll have to knock this cancer down again. My mother is still sick but no one seems to know exactly why. We're still waiting on some post-storm repairs, and calls to and from the insurance company just won't end. But I did arrive at my grandson's adorable program just as his group started to sing.

Things may not turn out the way I want them to, but that doesn't mean that God isn't good. It just means he has a different plan, a better plan—one that I may never understand on this earth. Yet I trust that he's a good, good father. Though my faith may waver, my confidence in his love for me never does.

Reflect and Respond

Do you ever feel like God is not on your side?

_____

_____

_____

What can you do to remind yourself of God's love for you even when his plans may not make sense to you?

_____

_____

_____

Don't forget to speak truth to yourself. God is faithful and good and loves you to the ends of the earth.

Nancy Holte is a freelance writer and speaker. She has been married for 44 years, and has three married sons and five adorable grandchildren. Nancy loves traveling, reading, sitting by the ocean, and spending time with her family. You can follow Nancy on Instagram or at www.nancyholte.com.

Day 19

Adamant Faith is Greater than

My Insecurities

SARAH GONZALEZ

I praise you, for I am fearfully and wonderfully made.
Wonderful are your works; my soul knows it very well.

Psalm 139:14 (NIV)

I have many unpleasant memories surrounding reading. I vividly remember the elementary school library. The sound of the red, heavy door creaking open. The pitter-patter of my classmates' small feet on the carpet becoming louder and faster as that door opened. The smiles on the other kids' faces as they raced to their favorite aisles. My classmates would excitedly pull books off the shelf and choose the ones they would check out with joy, showing them off to their friends. I didn't like book check-out days. In first grade, I checked out books based on whether their pages were glossy or matte. I liked the glossy pages.

I remember a time in fourth grade when our class read a science article aloud. The teacher had each of us read a paragraph. I anxiously counted down the page to find the paragraph I knew was mine to read aloud. I read it a few times to myself. When my turn came, I felt confident in my ability to read it, but totally missed the point of the article because I had only read a single paragraph. Every time I had to read aloud, I would feel my palms get sweaty and my stomach become uneasy. Anxiety ran through my whole body. Feelings of shame, insecurity, and embarrassment would bubble up inside me. I loved school because people were there, but I hated school because reading was there.

For many years, I felt embarrassed because I struggled with reading. I began to fear I was "stupid." And if that was true, what could I really accomplish? Who could I really be if I lacked simple academic skills? *I am who I am, and there's no changing it,* I told myself. Naturally, I started settling on who the world said I was. I began believing lies from the enemy: Lies that said I wasn't good enough, would never graduate college, and would never have a meaningful, successful career.

I am who I am. We have all thought that before, generally when we have fallen short of something. I have told myself these words when I've eaten too much cheesecake in one sitting, let the herbs I was definitely going to water die, or realized I was not as athletic as I wanted to be. *I am who I am. Can't change it.*

Maybe even worse than my lack of reading ability was the belief I adopted about myself: that I was dumb. That my brain was bad. *I am who I am, and there is no changing it,* I thought.

But the God we serve is an incredible one. He is strategic and good. I had quite the epiphany a few years back about my "bad brain."

Eight years ago, I started my first special education teaching position. I taught kids on the autism spectrum, and ironically (or maybe not at all) I was teaching language arts to kids who were reading far below grade level. I wasn't just okay at teaching reading. I was excellent! I had something that a lot of others didn't— relatability. I knew what it was like for those kids to struggle with reading and anxiety. I was able to sympathize with them and inspire them on a whole new level. The very thing that I hated most about myself as a child became my biggest asset as a teacher! How cool is God?!

1 Peter 2:9 says, *"But you are a chosen people, a royal priesthood, a holy nation, God's special possession, that you may declare the praises of him who called you out of darkness, and into his wonderful light."*

Sometimes I think back to the prayers I prayed as a child, pleading for a "smarter brain." I wonder if God was in Heaven thinking, *Daughter, wait! Your brain is beautiful, and it will accomplish beautiful things. Just wait.*

Now I have renewed confidence in myself because I know I am chosen, called, and special. I know there is an enormous plan for my life, and that God will use my amazing brain for amazing things. When I see myself starting to doubt my abilities, I remind myself: *I am who God says I am, and praise Jesus! There is no changing it.*

Reflect and Respond

When was a time that God took your painful situation and brought good from it?

_____

_____

_____

Sarah Gonzalez is a Christian stay-at-home mom. She loves writing, photography, and is a self-proclaimed quitter in recovery, on a mission to achieve her goals.

Day 20

Adamant Faith is Greater than

My Pain

ALISSA PERRY

Wait for the Lord; be strong and take heart and wait for the Lord.
Psalm 27:17 (NIV)

Scripture verses adorn my walls, hallways, and cupboard doors. They are next to mirrors, light switches and door frames. Nothing is off-limits—bedrooms, dining and living rooms, kitchen and bathrooms. God's word surrounds me wherever I turn. Verses are sometimes handwritten with care on white note cards, other times quickly scratched on yellow sticky notes, their fading, rolled edges showing their age.

All speak truth to my soul, but there are two verses placed next to my gray and blue paisley chair, the place where I go early every morning and sit to chat with my Lord. Deliberately, I maintain my sweet quiet time with Jesus. Before I'm overwhelmed with the chaos of five sets of busy feet and the chorus of voices calling out for me, I seek him out. I crave him. Before my world spins out of my control, as it always does, I *need* him.

I had always asked God to give me a testimony, a way to connect with others, to share deeply in their pain and grief, and then to celebrate the restoration he so amazingly provides. I just didn't know the true cost, how it would cut so deep. To feel close to death due to the most devastating of emotional wounds, inflicted by the one person on earth I thought loved me the most.

It was late on New Year's Eve when my husband finally told me about his long-term affair and his plan to leave. I didn't know how I would survive. We were stepping into a new year that was supposed to be brimming with beautiful possibilities for our family. Instead, in a moment, it felt like everything had been stolen from us. Adultery had never even been on my radar. I had thought we were a busy but happy family. Yet I was betrayed, blindsided, and suddenly discarded. Four months later, I learned they were expecting a baby together, due right around our fifteenth anniversary. My heart ripped open once again with the finality of the situation.

I felt as though nobody on earth could really understand my pain. I remember driving to church one morning, crying out, "I can't do this, God!" He quietly spoke to my heart, "I know. But I can."

And he has been faithful to bring me through every day. When I seek him, I find him. I hold to his promises, and he faithfully carries me through another day.

These verses near my chair are just two of God's beautiful and abundant promises, but they are the ones that speak to my heart daily—consistent reminders that he sees me and wants me to know he has good things in store.

The first verse is Proverbs 3: 5–6 (NIV), *"Trust in the Lord with all your heart, and lean not on your own understanding. In all your ways acknowledge Him, and He will make your paths straight."*

He knows every tear I cry, every prayer I speak, every thought in my heart. He knows my pain, and he reminds me again and again to *seek him, wait for him… hold on to him.* And when I can't seem to hold on any longer, he promises to hold onto me.

The beauty of God is that he chooses to never leave us nor forsake us—no matter how ugly life gets. No matter how raw or unruly. No matter how messy or morbid. He is with us in our worst possible, bottom-of-the-pit, drowning-in-our-sorrow moments.

And it is in those moments that we can either waste away in fear, bitterness, and despair, or choose to adamantly seek him. In those times, he teaches us things about his character we might not otherwise have a chance to learn. In those painful seasons, he is developing us into the people we are meant to become.

God knew the moment Satan began pulling at my husband's heart. God knew the years of deception even when I was blissfully unaware. God knew the exact moment my heart was going to shatter into a billion pieces. He already knew the intensity of my despair.

And he never left my side.

The second promise I claim every day is Psalm 27:13 (NIV): *"I remain confident of this; I will see the goodness of the Lord in the land of the living."*

He had already begun preparing my heart for these moments, these days, weeks, months and years. He had already been faithful to plant my family into a neighborhood that would support us in practical ways and satisfy our need for connection, and into a church of prayer warriors and close friends. Years in advance, he lined up friends who would simply be there, to encourage and to guide. He already had a plan to redeem what sin was about to destroy.

Our story continues to unfold. It isn't easy, and I don't have the final picture yet. But I will take another step forward in faith every day. Good things are coming. He has shown me glimpses already. He gives good gifts to his children, and we will not be forsaken.

Reflect and Respond

Are you willing to trust God with an *all-in* type of faith, no matter the messiness or pain of your current situation? If you are willing, how does that change the way you will approach the day ahead?

_____

_____

_____

How can you declare this faith through actions, words, and thoughts as you walk through the next 24 hours?

_____

_____

_____

Alissa Perry is the mother of five young children, following God's light through unexpectedly dark and turbulent territory. Previously basing her worth on her title as a wife, she is discovering that joy comes in being a daughter of the greatest King.

Day 21

Adamant Faith is Greater than

What I Lack

RENÉE GRIFFITH

*Therefore let us draw near with confidence to the throne of grace,
so that we may receive mercy and find grace to help in time of need.*

Hebrews 4:16 (NASB)

Some time ago, on the night of a confusing and particularly painful breakup, I lay awake in bed, firing off my questions to a dark and silent ceiling. *What could I have done to save this? Why was I too much but never enough?* My tears poured out to the point that they were pooling in my ears, so I turned over onto my stomach. Sobbing into my pillow, I moved beyond the point of asking for answers. *Just give me somewhere to put my faith, God,* I prayed. *Just give me something to hold on to.*

Out of nowhere, song lyrics filtered into my memory:

Before the throne of God above

I have a strong and perfect plea

A great High Priest whose name is Love

Who ever lives and pleads for me

At first, I was a little shocked: Honestly, I was expecting to hear a word from God containing hope for my present relational status, for him to tell me I would love again and that "my" person was still out there.

Instead, the Lord gave me himself.

My name is graven on His hands

My name is written on His heart

I know that while in Heav'n He stands

No tongue can bid me thence depart

I wanted a hand to hold—Jesus has my name engraved on his palms (Isaiah 49:16).

I wanted to be irreplaceable to someone—Jesus' love for me is as strong as death (Song of Solomon 8:6).

I wanted someone who would fight for me—Jesus Christ, the Righteous One, advocates for me before the Father (1 John 2:1).

I wanted the shadows—but Jesus had already given me the reality they represent.

Some of the lyrics from the song "Before the Throne of God Above,"* are based on Hebrews 4:14–16:

> *Therefore, since we have a great high priest who has passed through the heavens, Jesus the Son of God, let us hold fast our confession. For we do not have a high priest who cannot sympathize with our weaknesses, but One who has been tempted in all things as we are, yet without sin. Therefore let us draw near with confidence to the throne of grace, so that we may receive mercy and find grace to help in time of need.*

Jesus sympathizes with us in all our weaknesses; he gets us. When we think of adamant faith, we're likely to think of ourselves as the ones who need it. And we do. But let's remember that Jesus displays adamant faith, too: He never gives up on us and continues to remind us of all that his love has already won for us. Let's place our confidence in Christ's love-driven, finished work rather than in our desire for assurance regarding temporal things.

When our prospects for happiness disintegrate before our eyes, leaving us with nothing but shreds of unanswered questions, we can know that Jesus is still there, adamantly reminding us that our longings will be fulfilled ultimately by him. That alone should increase our confidence as we draw near to the throne of grace for the mercy we so desperately need.

All I could do the rest of that night was choke out the words until they became a song, then a whisper, and then a thought, until finally I fell asleep.

Reflect and Respond

Are you grasping at shadows and asking them to fill you more than God's reality? Ask the Lord to reveal to you whether you are misplacing your quest for satisfaction in the things of life rather than in the things of him. Then delve into Scripture passages that speak to the treasure we have in Christ, such as the following: Isaiah 42:1–9; Romans 5:1–5; Ephesians 1:3–23; Colossians 1:9–14.

_____

_____

_____

Are you purposing to exercise adamant faith in the big things but overlooking its value in the little things? Remember that no situation or desire is too small for God. Welcome him into the littlest thoughts of your day and ask him to lift your perspective to the things of heaven. As you do, watch your delight in him grow and color your desires for things here on earth.

_____

_____

_____

Renée Griffith is a writer and editor for *WorldView*, the Assemblies of God World Missions magazine. She served as an AGWM Missionary Associate in Moldova and Russia before earning her M.Div. at the Assemblies of God Theological Seminary. Now in Springfield, MO, she hails from Montana and enjoys burning pine-scented candles at all times of the year.

*"Before the Throne of God Above" was written by Charitie Lee Bancroft in 1863 and republished in 1871 (*The Baptist Hymn and Tunebook for Public Worship*) and in 1884 (Charles Spurgeon's *Our Hymn Book*). The song was redone in 1997 by Vicki Cook, with the most recent version in 2009 by Shane and Shane.

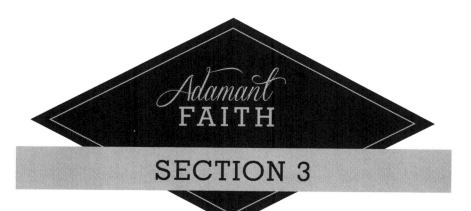

SECTION 3

Adamant Faith
Inspires Me to...

Day 22

Adamant Faith Inspires Me to

Keep Seeking

JEN SPIEGEL

Oh God, you are my God; earnestly I seek you; my soul thirsts for you;
my flesh faints for you, as in a dry and weary land where there is no water.

Psalm 63:1 (ESV)

From my spot at the top of the hill, I could see her coming. Slowly, one foot in front of the other, my five-year-old daughter plodded up the nearly vertical sand dune. Her face was all business: eyes on the path in front of her, toes sinking into the soft sand with each step, cheeks pink with effort.

As I waited for her to make it to the top, I took a moment to breathe deep. I felt a familiar whoosh of peace and wonder as I gazed out over Lake Michigan, vast and blue-gray as far as I could see. There's just something about big water that makes everything feel okay.

The moment was a stark contrast to the disaster my family had experienced the previous night, when in the peaceful stillness of a campground at 2 a.m., this same little girl sat straight up in the middle of the tent and whispered six words no parent ever wants to hear:

"I think I'm going to barf."

To avoid drawing bears to the campground, everything besides our bedding and clothing was tucked securely in our vehicle. Not a bowl or paper towel in sight. So even though she kindly gave us ten seconds of warning, all we could do to prepare for the onslaught was blindly grope for flashlights and mutter *please, Lord, no* while tripping over air mattresses and trying not to wake the other children.

It was just another chapter in the "why do we go camping?" saga that had become the theme of this particular trip. Gnats, rain, freezing nighttime temperatures that had us pulling hoods so tightly over our heads that only our nostrils were showing. And now—vomit.

Five minutes later, having stuffed my wool-stockinged feet into flip flops (always a good look), I awkwardly crept through the campground—one eye on the giant pile of unpleasantness in my arms, the other watching for the bear most certainly poised behind a nearby tree, readying itself to send me straight home to Jesus.

Although I somehow eluded the bear, it was still a particularly low moment—scrubbing regurgitated s'mores out of fleece blankets in a state park shower house, willing the water to wash the whole disaster away. In the moment, I wondered, *why do we do this to ourselves? Is seeking out a little time in nature really worth this mess?*

But standing at the top of the hill a few hours later, I couldn't help but giggle. That *mess,* I realized, would become a tale we'd tell until the end of time. And the view? *So* worth it.

My husband and I often joke that I was born in the wrong century, that my soul seems better suited for life in the Minnesota woods a few hundred years ago, my feet more amenable to a soft pair of deerskin moccasins than the rigid-soled Nikes I'd tossed into the grass before we began our dune climb that morning.

We don't get to choose the century in which we, in a gush of blood and water, enter into the great story of life. Likewise, the ways in which we find faith—and, perhaps even more so, *keep* it—are often unpredictable.

It's taken most of my life to accept that I don't always see God in the same places other people do. I encounter God far more often on a hiking path than in a steepled building. I hear whispers of love with my feet immersed in icy waves more clearly than when I'm reading an ancient text. I sense the existence of a wild and indefinable holiness in the stubborn weeds in my garden more often than in the familiar verses of a worship song.

Some people view faith as a rock to build upon. Some see it as a safe place to land in times of trouble. For others, faith is a carefully constructed, utterly defendable creed. Theologians have spent centuries defining it, debating whether it's earned or given, permanent or constantly in flux.

For me, someone who loves definitions, faith is frustratingly indefinable. It is less like words, more like water. It's silent yet somehow creates the most beautiful sounds and carves the most incredible paths. It's deeper than I can imagine and more complex than I can ever understand.

It changes with life's seasons—sometimes wildly alive, other times calm and quiet, sometimes even dried up. At times, it is solid and can be held. But mostly it slips through my fingers, leaving behind only a cool film of mystery.

Despite the times I've become so frustrated by doubts and questions that I've tried to shake it off completely, it lingers.

And even when I forget it's there, it quietly colors my world and directs my path.

As difficult as it is to define, for me, there is no life without faith.

As much of a mess as faith can become in this loud and murky world, as often as we might wonder if it's worth the wrestling and the doubting, an encounter with the God of constellations and ladybugs and big, wild waters is worth it. Every time.

It is when I'm face to face with tangled-up woods and untameable waters that I know this for sure: God is with us, and for us, and closer than we can comprehend.

As I grabbed my daughter's hand and walked the last few steps of the climb with her, I watched joy fill her little body and spill over as she bounced with renewed energy, so proud of how she'd simply kept going, not knowing exactly what she'd find at the top but believing it would be worth every step. How she wanted me to take twenty pictures of her posing at the top. How she knew this was a moment worth marking.

If your faith feels more like a desert than an ever-flowing stream, you're not alone. And it's okay.

Toss the things you can't define today into the grass, set your eyes on the path before you, and take a step.

Walk. Build. Heal. Play. Listen.

Pant your way to the top of a hill and feel the wide-eyed whoosh.

The struggle, the messiness, is worth it.

We shall seek. And we shall find.

Reflect and Respond

Have you struggled with what you've thought faith is "supposed" to look like? How has that idea changed throughout your life?

_____

_____

_____

When and where do you feel your faith come alive? How can you create more space in your life for opportunities to experience communion with God within that context?

_____

_____

_____

Jen Spiegel is an editor and advisor for Bridging the Gap's writing team, where she shares her passion for honest storytelling and helping women discover the healing power of writing. She enjoys date nights, outdoor adventures with her family, and curling up with a good book and a one-eyed dog named Finn.

Day 23

Adamant Faith Inspires Me to
Keep Showing Up

AMBER GERSTMANN

*Being confident of this, that he who began a good work in you
will carry it on to completion until the day of Christ Jesus.*

Philippians 1:6

"Wow, this is a really long distance," I said.

My husband glanced at me with a puzzled expression. "You nervous? I thought you run this all the time?" he said.

"I do; I've run twice this distance. *I have just never seen it stretched out like this...*"

Years ago, I somewhat accidentally stumbled into running. I cannot think of a more perfect word picture as I was definitely clumsy about it in every way. It happened in fits and starts, while plodding out the time on the treadmill at my local gym, my feet sounding like a herd of cattle clattering with every step that landed heavily on the spinning, stationary track. I was new to this, and I was not graceful.

I didn't mind, though. I was too enthralled with the idea that I was actually running. I was also preoccupied, dealing with a heavy heart and anxiety that seemed to have arrived out of nowhere. Tending to my soul needs in an effort to heal was no small task. Working through my thoughts and feelings on the treadmill was messy but helpful. These two clumsy journeys overlapped, and I started referring to runs as Treadmill Time with Jesus.

Years earlier, I had myself completely convinced that I would never be able to run a full mile in my lifetime. And when I first crossed that milestone, I suddenly became "that weird lady at the gym," hopping off the treadmill with my arms in the air, "spirit fingers" raised as I did a little dance.

Most of the time, we cannot perceive the new things that God is doing in us on our own. We cannot see—in real time—the healing work of growth he does in us. All we can see is perhaps that first mile breakthrough.

Before I knew it, I was running several miles a week during Treadmill Time with Jesus, and I signed up for my first 5k race. Feeling new and uncertain, my husband and I were driving the course the night before the event when I was surprised at how long the distance looked and commented on it. *All* my running up to that point had been from a stationary visual vantage point.

While I have never heard the audible voice of the Lord, at that moment my heart heard him say, "In the same way, you have *no idea* how far I have taken you in this healing journey. On the other side of this struggle with anxiety, you will be amazed at the *miles* and *miles* and *miles* that I have brought you."

I have literally run more than a thousand cumulative miles since that day, but this word from the Lord has remained in the forefront of my mind when I'm waiting on breakthrough or healing. Adamant faith inspires me to look to his ultimate sovereignty over all things and my life in particular. His promises to make me more like Christ keep me showing up day after day on the spiritual treadmill, pounding the pavement of an abiding life in Christ. He is good to his word. At all times, he is doing far more *in me* than I can see.

Make no mistake, we are never stationary in our walk with the Lord. And whatever he has begun in our lives, he will be faithful to complete.

Reflect and Respond

Do you have a prayer for healing or change that you have been holding before the Lord for an extended season? How does it encourage your faith to meditate on the idea that He is working even when you cannot see?

_____

_____

_____

Take some time to consider how far God has brought you on your own faith journey.

_____

_____

_____

Amber Gerstmann is wife to Trevor and momma of four. She's a worship leader, Bible/theology teacher, runner, coffee snob, and foodie. Amber loves to geek out on all things music and theology. One can typically find her chasing her littles, dabbling in photography, or singing (loudly) at the piano.

Day 24

Adamant Faith Inspires Me to

Sing of the Faithful

SANDY MCKEOWN

I will sing of the Lord's great love forever;
with my mouth I will make your faithfulness
known through all generations.

Psalm 89:1 (NIV)

My husband, a conductor for a daily passenger train, is often an unofficial tour guide for commuters as well. One day a gentleman who had recently moved to the region questioned how to get to an area casino. My funnyman, not knowing the exact location of the casino but the general direction, suggested the gamester drive to the main highway toward the casino and follow the Buicks. My guy was quite sure the drivers of said cars would lead this newcomer to his desired destination.

The man was skeptical, but agreed to try it on his day off.

The next time the gentleman was riding my husband's train, he found him: "You were right! It worked! All I had to do was follow the Buicks!"

Who do *you* follow to reach your desired destination?

My husband and I met a couple almost 40 years ago that would become lifelong, worthy-to-be-followed friends.

I was a young mom yearning for friends when I ended up in the crying room with our firstborn on our first visit to a new church in a new city. Inside was a friendly lady with a baby about the same age as mine. She and her husband had tried for years to have a second child but were unable to, she informed me. Through adoption, this child was the answer to their prayers.

We became fast friends, and through the years this couple always loved, always cared. They babysat when we had no money to pay a sitter. They hosted our kids and me when my husband was out of town for work on Thanksgiving and Christmas. As a nurse, my new friend was my back-up coach for unpredictable labor and deliveries. She called daily to check on me when she knew I was struggling while my husband traveled.

Through this entire relationship, we watched as the boy who was the answer to their prayers grew from innocent childhood to mischievous pre-teen, diagnosed with mental illness, to troubled teen.

We watched this couple pray as their son became hooked on drugs.

We watched this couple pray as their son began stealing to purchase the drugs.

We watched our friends pray as they visited their son in jail.

We watched as they prayed for a job for their once-incarcerated son.

We watched as they prayed for their son's girlfriend's pregnancy.

We watched as they prayed—and selflessly cared for—their son's first child… and second child…and third.

And we watched as the judge took the children away from their parents, as they were adopted out-of-state, and as their grandparents said their goodbyes.

With another move, our visits lessened, but last summer they arrived for a quick stopover. After their overnight stay, we were walking them through the garage entrance when my friend turned to her husband and exclaimed, "Wait a minute! We haven't prayed with them!"

And the four of us—my husband and I, and our friends of almost 40 years—immediately stopped beside our washer and dryer, forced into a tight circle in the tiny space.

And they prayed.

They entered into his presence with ease.

They spoke of his blessings.

They worshipped him.

They adored him.

And as we stood and soaked in their conversation with their Lord, I heard two people pray who had never given up on their son and never walked away from their Father.

Certainly doubt entered when a son who was an answer to their prayers became a son who was the source of unfathomable grief.

Jesus himself, while hanging on the cross, cried out: *"My God, my God, why have you forsaken me?"*

Our human friends probably had a similar moment in private, but they never wavered in public.

Their faith isn't based on their feelings. Their faith is based on their knowledge of him. They have modeled for me a faith that doesn't stop. A faith that compels them to *keep serving publicly* no matter what is happening privately.

They have demonstrated a relentless faith to countless people that makes my faith pale in comparison.

They have *sung of the Lord's great love…with their mouths they make his faithfulness known to all generations.*

As I ponder their faithfulness, it urges me to grow mine. Oh, that I would someday have faith like my long-time friends: a faith that doesn't look down at my circumstances during the hard journey, but keeps my eyes upon Jesus *despite* the exhausting journey.

Reflect and Respond

How do you intentionally grow your faith?

_____

_____

_____

Are you following the right people to reach your desired destination?

_____

_____

_____

Sandy McKeown and her husband raised five children, three with extra challenges. She has been published in several anthologies and is a speaker for women's groups, men's groups, college classrooms, and church services. Sandy also mentors women, helping them discover raising challenging children and keeping their marriages strong simultaneously is possible.

Day 25

Adamant Faith Inspires Me to

Press On

JANAE LENNING

Jesus Christ is the same yesterday and today and forever.
Hebrews 13:8 (NIV)

For the last eight and a half years, I've been on a rollercoaster journey to being diagnosed with fibromyalgia. Following a bad skiing accident and then a car accident, the pain that's now spread throughout my body has been consistent and constant, pretty even as far as its presence in my life. But the emotional side of things? Now that's another story.

The list goes on and on of people who have promised me some kind of relief or healing: Doctors, nurses, specialists, physical therapists, and even random people who've found "the solution."

"Just try this!" "My cousin did this and feels so much better!" "It's amazing how much [insert health or pseudo-health treatment here] works!" "Instant relief!"

And I've tried it all. I'm always willing to take a shot at feeling better. But what about when we've tried it all and our painful situation remains? When spiritual platitudes are thrown into the mix, it only makes things messier.

"You need to have more faith!" "God is just trying to teach you something through this…" "I know that God wants to heal you today!" "Claim the healing that we're

promised in Jesus' name!" "Don't let negative thoughts keep you from getting what you desire."

In the middle of living with chronic illness and praying for deliverance that never arrives, where does faith come in? When the God of miracles doesn't open the door and give us the gift we're looking for, is he still the one we've put our hope and faith in? Do we still have faith in Jesus who is the same yesterday, today, and forever when all three seem bleak?

I've heard many times that faith is the key to getting what you've been asking for to appear. At the same time, I know deep in my bones that faith is so much more than that. The way God has walked with me through every step of this journey has taught me that faith *must* be more. Faith is deeper than a solution, a miracle, or a way out. True faith doesn't give up when we don't get what we want.

The outcome of our petitions isn't the basis for faith. The basis for our faith is the character of God. Who God is is more than enough for us to place our lives wholeheartedly in his hands, trusting him no matter what the outcome.

Adamant faith remains and sustains when nothing else does. Adamant faith is the foundation we can stand upon when the walls fall down and there are no options left. When you don't have any choice but to put one foot in front of the other, faith is what forms the ground beneath our feet. It spurs us on and reassures us that God is still who he always has been, no matter our circumstances.

I've come to accept that unless a miracle happens, fibromyalgia will always be a part of my life. I've realized that it's only with a deep-seated faith that I'm able to accept this reality. When I see that God is good, kind, loving, and merciful—even in the midst of pain—I can walk forward with the cross that has been laid on my back.

The cross of Jesus is what gives us the strength to acknowledge that our deepest pain doesn't cancel out the loving character of God. There's nothing we can go through that is stronger than his love. We're never outside of his kindness. So even when we are blinded by our struggles, this everlasting love leads us on and inspires the kind of faith that presses on through the storm.

This pressing-on kind of faith is strong enough to recognize the reality of our broken world and our broken lives and still declare the goodness of God. We can still seek joy. We can look forward and trust that God is going to redeem every painful part of our story. We can take that next step without worrying about who will be alongside us.

No matter what happens, our faith can be sustained by the everlasting goodness of our God. We can press on, ultimately resting in the fact that our faith can be as deep as the love of God, which is stronger than anything we could encounter in this world. Let us throw off the weight of spiritual guilt when our prayers aren't answered simply. Faith in our God can handle every hardship because he can handle every hardship.

Reflect and Respond

What attributes of Jesus can you hold on to in the midst of trials or uncertainty?

_____

_____

_____

How can faith encourage us when our prayers go unanswered?

_____

_____

_____

Janae Lenning currently lives and works in Fez, Morocco. Studying and teaching in France led her to North Africa, where she seeks to find joy and love of God amidst the struggle of living with fibromyalgia.

Day 26

Adamant Faith Inspires Me to

Forgive

KRISTEN LARSON

Make allowance for each other's faults, and forgive anyone who offends you.
Remember, the Lord forgave you, so you must forgive others.

Colossians 3:13 (NLT)

Last spring, I found out I have SIBO (small intestinal bacterial overgrowth) as well as some other significant food sensitivities that resulted in chronic fatigue, upset stomach, and anxiety. The treatment my doctor gave me was a *dramatic* change in my diet. It meant eliminating all kinds of things from my diet (like dairy, nuts, grains, and coffee, among other things) which translated into making all my meals from scratch. The convenience of grabbing a pre-made meal at the grocery store was gone.

The first month was the worst. I had to reinvent my life and cut commitments from my schedule so that I would have time to cook. Most of my life became, and remains, split between the office and my kitchen.

But what was just as difficult was enduring the passive judgment I got from people. Until you have a food sensitivity or you're put on a strict diet, you really can't understand how difficult it is. And I get that. I used to be that person.

One day while I was out grabbing ingredients for lunch, I ran into a friend. She knew the diet I was on and began asking questions about it. As we talked, I sensed a condescending tone.

She asked, "You're not supposed to eat that, right? That's not on your diet." Little did she know that one ingredient was one of the few items I had left to phase out. I had eliminated so much from my diet already. I just wasn't ready for that step yet.

By the time our conversation was over, I felt like a failure. Instead of feeling the victory of how far I had come and how much better I was feeling, I felt like I wasn't doing well enough. It felt like all my victories were chopped down in front of me.

I felt deflated. I was upset. *Who does she think she is? Why did she have to prod so much? Couldn't she mind her own business?*

But no more than a few minutes passed until God reminded me of Colossians 3:13, which tells us to *make allowance for each other's faults, and forgive anyone who offends you. Remember, the Lord forgave you, so you must forgive others.*

I felt God saying to me, *Kristen, make allowance for her faults. Forgive her for offending you. Remember, I forgave you. I expect you to do the same for others.*

It's easy to hear what the Lord says. It's harder to obey it.

After talking with God for a few minutes and really thinking over what he was asking of me, the blinders fell from my eyes. As I stepped back from the offense and looked at the big picture, I could see that my friend didn't mean to hurt me. The questions she had asked were innocent, and her attitude was innocent as well. There was no way she could have known all that was going on behind the scenes in my life, just as I couldn't know everything about hers! How often do we assume the worst in our relationships? How many times have we let our pain put a wedge between us and someone we care about?

As I re-evaluated our conversation, I realized that she never actually said anything hurtful. The only reason my defenses rose up was because I was reminded of how hard this change has been for me and how I'm still just getting used to it.

The Lord commanded me to make an allowance for my friend's faults. I needed to brush this one off my shoulders and move on without blaming her or staying mad. My feelings wanted me to believe one story, but the Lord commanded me to believe another.

Remember what Jesus did for us.

When someone offends us, we need to be steadfast in what Jesus tells us to do. We need to hold firm to what he teaches. We need to have faith that is so adamant, so uncompromising, that we put his truth before anything else.

Reflect and Respond

Who's offended you recently? It may be a friend, a parent, a coworker or a spouse. As you read Colossians 3:13, does it make you think differently about the situation?

_____

_____

_____

How can you practice forgiveness today?

_____

_____

_____

In what ways can you practice adamant faith?

_____

_____

_____

Kristen Larson loves encouraging others by sharing testimonies of God's faithfulness wherever she gets the chance. She has written devotionals for Barbour Publishing, was a blog contributor for the Faith Radio Network, and is currently working her dream job at Bethany House Publishers. She is the author of AbideTrustBelieve.com, an online devotional.

Day 27

Adamant Faith Inspires Me to

Love Others

RACHAEL ADAMS

Faith by itself, if it is not accompanied by action is dead.

James 2:17 (NIV)

When do you feel most loved? I have been pondering this question a lot lately. As Christians, we are called to love the Lord God with all of our heart, with all of our soul, and with all of our mind, and to love our neighbor as ourselves (Matthew 22:37–40). This command to love can seem daunting at times and, for me, often results in being paralyzed with inactivity.

We all yearn to hear the three words, "I love you." However, I wonder if hearing them also translates to believing them? If someone tells us they love us, but doesn't show us they love us, does it carry the same weight? Unfortunately, it's often the moments when we don't feel loved that are the easiest to recall.

I was chatting with my husband about this topic recently, and he suggested that in order for someone to feel loved, they must see ongoing action that backs up the words. Consistently being present to meet another person's need makes them feel most loved.

Reflecting on my marriage and other relationships in my life, I think he is right. As much as I long to hear the words, "I love you," I long much more for my husband to show me he loves me through his actions. It is not enough for him to say he does or to show me once or twice. The reality is, I need him to constantly express his love through action in order for me to feel loved.

I feel loved when he greets me with a smile after a long day at work, when he sets down his phone to look me in the eye and listen to my day, when he winks at me from across the room, when he sends me a text to tell me he is thinking about me, when he compliments the meal I made and offers to do the dishes, and when he draws me a bath and lays out a book for me to read when he knows I need some rest and relaxation.

My husband loves me well by noticing me and caring enough to pay attention to meet my needs. Sometimes in big ways, but mostly in the small ordinary everyday ways. His actions reveal he sees me and values me. This is also what he needs from me. So do my children, so do my parents, so do my friends, and so do all the people we encounter in this life.

Love is more than a feeling; it is a verb. It is something we give, something we do. God knows this well because God is love. God created us because he loved us. God sent Jesus because he loved us. Jesus died on the cross because he loved us. Now we are to love because he first loved us.

God not only tells us he loves us in his word, but he follows through with action. In response, we are to show our love to him by loving others through our actions. While we may be tempted to believe we must earn God's love, this couldn't be further from the truth. It is faith that leads us into salvation, but our active obedience proves our faith is genuine. Scripture tells us that faith by itself, if it is not accompanied by action, is dead (James 2:17). True faith results in deeds of loving service.

This concept of faith expressed in loving action is displayed beautifully by four men in the Gospel of Mark. We read in chapter 2 about Jesus teaching in a home in Capernaum. Mark tells us four men carried a paralytic man on his mat to be healed by Jesus, but because the crowd was so large, they could not reach him. Desperate to see their friend healed, they made an opening in the roof and lowered the man down to Jesus. When Jesus saw their faith, he healed the paralytic man both spiritually and physically. It wasn't his faith that impressed Jesus. Instead, it was the collective faith of his friends who brought him to Jesus. Their faith led them to loving service and hence healed the man on the mat.

For better or for worse, our faith affects others. We can not compel another person to become a Christian, but our words, actions, and love can demonstrate the power of Christ's love and make an impact on the lives of those around us. This realization causes me to reflect on my own actions or lack thereof. When was the last time I had such a longing to see my fellow man's sins forgiven that I took extreme steps to help someone find Jesus, as these four men did? When have I displayed an urgency in my heart to stop at nothing to lay my friend at the feet of Jesus? To do everything in my power to get them into his presence because of my love for the Lord and for mankind?

The paralytic man's need moved his friends to compassionate action. What about us? When we recognize someone's need, let's move past our tendency to remain paralyzed with inactivity. Rather, let's react in loving service to meet the need either by ourselves or with the help of others who are also concerned. Together, our faith should go beyond lip service and result in tangible service.

We show the love of Christ by being present with our families, feeding the hungry, inviting the stranger, listening to the lonely, caring for the orphan, praying for the sick, visiting the widow, providing shelter and any other action we take with pure and servant-hearted motives. It simply requires following the Lord's lead to selflessly be aware and attentive to the needs of those God has surrounded us with.

While only God's love can truly satisfy the longing in our hearts, he has placed us on this planet for a purpose. We can be the answer to someone's prayer through our faith in action. Let's live with the mindset of demonstrating our faith in God through our loving service to others. In doing so, we may even make someone's list of when they felt most loved. We may make someone feel loved for the very first time. Or, best of all, we may lead them to God, who will make them feel loved for all of eternity.

Reflect and Respond

How can you put your faith in action through loving service today?

_____

_____

_____

Rachael Adams is a writer, speaker, podcaster, and founder of The Love Offering. Her heart's desire is to encourage women to realize their God-given purpose and to embolden them to move into the world through compassionate action. Rachael and her husband live in Kentucky with their two children. Connect with her online at www.rachaelkadams.com or on Facebook and Instagram @rachaeladamsauthor.

Day 28

Adamant Faith Inspires Me to

Get Back Up

BECKY MEYERSON

So do not throw away this confident trust in the Lord.
Remember the great reward it brings you! Patient endurance is what you need now,
so that you will continue to do God's will.
Then you will receive all that he has promised.

Hebrews 10:35–36 (NLT)

In 2008, Heather Dorniden took a terrible fall during the Big Ten 600-meter final in Minneapolis that would have been the end of the story for most people. But what she did next was surprising and inspiring.

Heather was in first place when she fell to the track . . . hard.

In the moments before she was able to get back up and continue the race, other runners passed her until there was a gap of 30 meters.

Heather later remembered, "After I fell, it was as if a vacuum had sucked all the energy out of the place; then, as I got up and started to gain momentum, it was like a crescendo of noise and excitement, all the way to the finish line. I thought, 'Wouldn't it be cool if I caught them all?'"[2]

---

2 Yarina, Brent. "A race to remember: 'I had no idea I fell like that' in inspirational 2008 run." *Big Ten Network*. 3 June 2015. Web. https://btn.com/2015/06/03/a-race-to-remember-i-had-no-idea-i-fell-like-that-in-inspirational-2008-run/

And that's what she did. She only had one lap to make her nearly impossible comeback, but she persevered and passed each runner one at a time to finish in first place.

In the years that have followed, thousands of people have watched her courageous race on YouTube. The grainy VHS video reminds the downtrodden and hopeless that it's worth getting up and rising above adversity every single time.

This is what the writer of Hebrews (the coach) is telling his readers (the runners): *"So do not throw away this confident trust in the Lord. Remember the great reward it brings you! Patient endurance is what you need now, so that you will continue to do God's will. Then you will receive all that he has promised"* (Hebrews 10:35–36, NLT).

Earlier in their faith journey, these believers had endured hardship and persecution with confident faith, but now they were close to throwing their trust in God away.

The writer of Hebrews offers encouragement in the same way Heather's track coach and her parents did while cheering from the bleachers. "Don't give up! Stand up and keep running because you just don't know what might happen."

Before you toss your faith out the door, remember two things:

First, faith doesn't shatter. Pat Barrett sings in his song *Into Faith I Go*, "faith is not some fragile thing that shatters when we walk through something hard."

That is biblical truth! 1 Corinthians 13:13 tells us that there are three things that remain—faith, hope and love. The Greek word for *remain* means that it abides, survives, endures, and lasts.

We may think that our faith has shattered and been destroyed when we are at the bottom of life, but faith remains—it lasts forever. Don't measure what you believe by what you are experiencing. You may not "feel" faith in your life, but that doesn't mean it isn't still there. Faith is the enabling and enduring power of God given to you at salvation.

When you fall, fail, endure hardships, and want to give up, keep your eyes on Jesus who is the pioneer and perfecter of your faith (Hebrews 12:2).

Second, give faith time to work. Faith and patient endurance are partners. In the original Greek, "patient endurance" is exemplified by a person who is under a very heavy load but who has resolved to remain steadfast in faith.

Part of practicing faith is persevering in it. Trials and tests are not meant to be something we speed through, checking boxes along the way. They are designed to challenge our faith so we become mature and dependent on Jesus.

So, don't give up and throw it all away. Follow the examples given by pioneers of faith that are cheering for us. The Message phrases it this way:

> *Do you see what this means—all these pioneers who blazed the way, all these veterans cheering us on? It means we'd better get on with it. Strip down, start running—and never quit! No extra spiritual fat, no parasitic sins. Keep your eyes on Jesus, who both began and finished this race we're in. Study how he did it. Because he never lost sight of where he was headed—that exhilarating finish in and with God—he could put up with anything along the way: Cross, shame, whatever (Hebrews 12:1–3).*

Hang in there! Never give up. No matter how skinned your knees are from falling on unforgiving tarmac, you can finish your race strong. Be the runner who is tough, resistant, persistent, obstinate, stubborn, and tenacious. Refuse to let go of what you believe. Be a resilient, enduring woman of faith.

Reflect and Respond

Have you known people who once walked in faith but let discouragement turn them sour? After walking away from faith, did their life improve or deteriorate? Take a few minutes to pray for them today and ask the Lord if there is a practical way you can show them his love.

_____

_____

_____

Are you tempted to give up on dreams God has given you? Are you discouraged because your prayers seem to be hitting a brick wall? What steps can you take today to strengthen your faith so you can get back up and continue running?

_____

_____

_____

Becky Meyerson is passionate about writing and teaching from the Word of God. Her heart is to see women flourish in every season of life. To encourage and empower women to live abundantly, she writes free Bible reading plans, Bible studies, blogs, and speaks on healthy thinking. Find more at www.beckymeyerson.com.

Day 29

Adamant Faith Inspires Me to
Demonstrate Hope and Mercy

AMINTA GEISLER

God blesses those who are merciful, for they will be shown mercy.
Matthew 5:7 (NLT)

I was almost home from the grocery store when I saw an elderly woman lying in a snowbank. She was flat on her back and unable to get up, so I pulled over to help. As I got closer, I could smell the alcohol. It radiated from her body, as did the stench of body odor. Her clothes were dirty and far too thin for this blustery winter day.

"Are you hurt, ma'am?" I asked as I squatted down to help. Her reply was slurred and unintelligible.

"Can you stand up?"

She moaned in response.

I slid my arm under her shoulder and took her hand in mind. "On the count of three, let's try to get you out of this snow...1...2...3..." I pulled her up with every ounce of strength I had, but to no avail. She contributed zero effort, and my feeble attempt to lift her failed.

I wasn't sure what to do. *Had she hit her head? Was she badly injured or just drunk? How would I ever get her off the ground?*

Her moans got louder.

"It's ok, ma'am." I tried to comfort her. "I'm here to help. Let's try again, okay?" *Help me Jesus,* I whispered as I pulled again, but it was no use. I couldn't move her.

Cars were driving past me in a steady procession. Some slowed down to gawk, but most kept right on cruising. I felt helpless. Finally, a man pulled over to assist me and between the two of us, we were able to lift her out of the snow and carry her to a nearby bench.

I sat down beside her and started picking snow and dirt out of her hair. A passerby hollered out, "Do you want me to call 911?"

"Yes, please!" It hadn't even occurred to me to call for help.

I took the woman's icy hand in mine and asked, "What is your name?"

She looked me straight in the eyes and said clear as a bell, "Hope."

My eyes filled with tears. If I had ever met someone who should be without hope, it was this woman. Yet, she had confidently declared her name to me when all other words failed her.

Hope.

I took a deep breath and asked, "Can I pray for you?"

She nodded, so I closed my eyes and prayed for blessing, healing, and freedom over her life. Tears ran down her face as I said amen.

The ambulance still hadn't arrived, so I grabbed some crackers from my van. Just as Hope started to eat, I saw the flashing lights. I felt relieved, at first, but the responders were less than sympathetic. I'm sure the daily responsibilities of the job had made them calloused over time, but it was difficult to watch how harshly they treated her.

I stayed and held Hope's hand until she was loaded inside the ambulance. One of the paramedics tried to give me back the crackers, but I said she could keep them.

"What a waste," he said to me as he slammed the doors. I couldn't help thinking that he was utterly wrong.

Mercy, no matter the recipient, is never a waste. There is not a person on earth that is unworthy of loving kindness. Not one. No matter what mistakes they have made, no matter how lost they have become, no matter how broken they are.

Each person is counted precious and worthy of mercy in God's eyes. My life is proof! God showed me mercy when I deserved judgement, and his mercy has given me the courage to love others who are undeserving. Because of my adamant faith in Christ, I am inspired to be a person who freely gives mercy to people like Hope.

Reflect and Respond

James 2:13 (NLT) tells us, *"There will be no mercy for those who have not shown mercy to others. But if you have been merciful, God will be merciful when he judges you."* Think about the last time you saw someone who was in need. Was your response one of mercy, judgment, or both?

_____

_____

_____

What is one tangible way that you can show mercy to someone this week?

_____

_____

_____

Aminta Geisler is a writer, speaker, and podcaster. She is passionate about sharing God's love and is determined to chase after Jesus no matter the cost. She recently founded Reckless Abandon Ministries, a nonprofit dedicated to fighting youth hunger and homelessness. Read more at amintageisler.com.

Day 30

Adamant Faith Inspires Me to

Love Wholeheartedly

ANGIE KUTZER

And now these three remain: faith, hope and love.
But the greatest of these is love.

1 Corinthians 13:13

While decorating my home for an upcoming Valentine's Day, I decided to choose some meaningful words to incorporate in my décor.

I settled on 1 Corinthians 13:13, *"And now these three remain: faith, hope and love. But the greatest of these is love."*

I began thinking about these words more deeply, as I organized pink hearts and sparkly things to adorn my little part of the world, which I share with the people I deeply love. I pondered how love really is the center of life. Without love, hope might be lost, and without love, there wouldn't be anything to have faith in. Truly, the greatest of those is love!

Jesus' model of unconditional love is unbeatable. He showed us how to love the people around us the people around us as ourselves, regardless of who those people are. Jesus modeled self-sacrifice for the benefit of others. He lived a life of immeasurable love and unwavering faith.

Jesus was constantly surrounded by people who were sick, unclean, and of ill repute, but he never seeming to think twice about spending his days with them.

Jesus had adamant faith that as God led his path to intersect with those of many other people, God would guide him through every situation he encountered.

Are you capable of mustering faith so solid that it will enable you to love and live like Jesus?

God created everything to coexist, and all of creation thrives on love. The proof is all around us.

The plant that is cared for blooms. The pet that is loved loves in return. The homeless individual who finds good fortune shares that good fortune with others in need. The inmate who meets Jesus while incarcerated begins a Bible study group to spread the love of Jesus to those around him.

The greatest of these is love.

Adamant faith reminds us to love even when it is tough.

Jesus teaches us to love the seemingly unlovable because love heals, because love spreads. Because love wins.

My adamant faith and the love that Jesus Christ has given me have enabled me to overflow with love in order to spread that love to those who may need it most.

Jesus calls me to volunteer in the local food pantry and smile my brightest smile at all who enter. While there, the Holy Spirit provides opportunities for me to frolic with the children and blow bubbles and laugh as their guardians are blessed with food. While spreading the love of Jesus there, I am moved to live more frugally and to give more openly. While there, I meet the hard-working young carpenter who does not have safe and stable work boots, and I am moved to spread the love of God by providing him with boots. While serving there, I learn that some people cannot accept canned food, simply because they don't own a can opener; and I later use God's blessings to meet this need by purchasing some.

While there serving God's people and spreading love, I also find love. I receive it in the smile of a lonely widow. I see Jesus in the father and child, straight off the street, who share a bond greater than most fathers and children I have ever met. I feel love and appreciation flowing through the hugs of the recipients and the prayers of my fellow volunteers. I recognize the love flowing from the mouths of those who come through the door, as they greet the volunteers by name and humbly accept the gifts offered.

The greatest of these is Love.

Love modeled by the adamant, unwavering faith of Jesus Christ.

Love grounded in the promises of God and guided by the Holy Spirit.

Love that recognizes need and opens our hearts in a way that they will never close again.

May you embrace that love and share your adamant faith and your blessings, each and every day, in every opportunity that arises!

Reflect and Respond:

When have you felt the unshakable love of God?

_____

_____

_____

What can you do to spread the faith, hope, and love of Jesus to someone in need today?

_____

_____

_____

Angie Kutzer has been authoring faith-filled short stories for more than five years. Her ministry, FromMyLifeToYourHeart, started out of a passion to share her life experiences and her faith. FromMyLifeToYourHeart's mission is to "Inspire Good Choices, Perseverance, and Forgiveness." Angie is also currently attending Luther Seminary, working toward her graduate degree. She plans to become a deacon and work with nonprofit organizations in that capacity. Find Angie's blog and more at www.frommylifetoyourheart.com.

Day 31

Adamant Faith Inspires Me to
Extend a Hand in Friendship

KRISTIN DEMERY

… We throw open our doors to God and discover at the same moment that he has already thrown open his door to us. We find ourselves standing where we always hoped we might stand—out in the wide open spaces of God's grace and glory, standing tall and shouting our praise.

Romans 5:2 (MSG)

The kitchen was bustling, food sizzling as conversations hummed. Women were grouped around the island and table, spilling over into the living and dining rooms. The multi-hued array of spices redolent in the air reflected the various cultures represented in the room.

It was the first self-proclaimed "feast," part of an endeavor dreamed up by my friend Samantha. She and her husband Andrew had moved back to the area to work with the community's burgeoning refugee and immigrant population, and her idea for a multicultural community cookbook—proceeds which would go to benefit a refugee-related ministry—had been set in motion a couple of months earlier. After the initial planning meeting, the group decided to host feasts to sample the recipes featured in the cookbook.

As an observer tasked with writing down the recipes and stories about the women who made them, I sat in the living room with my mouth watering. Women from Somalia, China, Iraq, Mexico, and the United States mingled with one another, discussing recipes and children, husbands and jobs. I watched as Fartun's youngest daughter, impeccably dressed but missing her hijab, moseyed over to where I sat with my computer resting on my lap. Elbowing me aside, she pushed the buttons repeatedly while I laughingly tried to distract her, trying to focus despite the cacophony of voices.

Some were familiar faces, others newcomers. I'd met Anoosha, originally from India, on New Year's Eve. Seeing her again, I congratulated her on her pregnancy as her laughter bubbled over.

In the kitchen, Amna was making dolma. When I offered to help, she put me to work pulling grape leaves carefully from a jar, rinsing them to remove acidity. Originally from Iraq, she has a master's degree in microbiology; her husband has a doctorate and teaches environmental science. As we spooned the rice and meat mixture on to the leaves, her daughters flitted through the kitchen before rushing back to play with friends.

At every feast, the women worked together to create a few dishes while others were prepared in advance. One of my favorites was Carmen's dumplings. Originally from China, she and her mother patiently let everyone have a turn creating them, handing out small circles of dough to be filled and crimped on the edges. She showed us a few times and pressed the edges together in a way that turned out perfectly. My own efforts were more wobbly, but she remained encouraging in her praise.

Looking around, I was in awe of the sense of community represented. Samantha and Andrew aren't trying to share their faith in the way I understood it growing up. There wasn't a pulpit or whiteboard present, no Bibles lying open, no attempts to talk about sins or grace. They weren't trying to present a perfect vision of our faith and the theological underpinnings that support it. Instead, they were simply extending a hand in friendship—even as they acknowledge that the reason they love so well is because they are Jesus-followers.

Reflecting on those truths, I'm reminded of a conversation I had with Anoosha on that cold winter day in late December. When asked how she ended up in Minnesota, she said that her husband came to the area for a master's degree program. It was lonely when she first arrived.

"In India, it was so hot that in the evenings, everyone would throw open their windows and doors. It was noisy and there were lots of kids around," she said. "Here, everyone is behind closed doors."

I found myself nodding in understanding. When my husband and I moved into our first home, we only knew a few neighbors. I could imagine how isolating it would feel to move to a new country. Shooting a smile over to Samantha, Anoosha said that things had gotten better once she'd met a friend. Before we left that evening, she took selfies with my 3-year-old, two faces beaming at the camera.

Anoosha's longing for the open doors and homes she experienced in her childhood is something that God himself offers to us. I love how The Message puts it: *"We throw open our doors to God and discover at the same moment that he has already thrown open his door to us."* Our hospitality, our love and concern for others, is simply a reflection of what God has already done for us.

I've found that some of the deepest conversations about faith are only made possible through living an open-door life where friendship comes first and our expectations are secondary. In friendship, Jesus can be reflected—not in a communion cup or the lyrics of a hymn—but in the faces of his followers, the church, loving neighbors as well as they love themselves.

Reflect and Respond

In what ways does our faith encourage us to cultivate hospitality?

_____

_____

_____

Who can you extend a hand of friendship to today?

_____

_____

_____

Kristin Demery is a wife, mom, and coauthor of several books, including *The One Year Daily Acts of Kindness* devotional (Tyndale, 2017) and *100 Days of Kindness* (Tyndale, 2019). Kristin loves staying up way too late, spending sun-soaked days at Madeline Island with her family, sipping campfire mochas, thrifting, and gift giving. Find more from Kristin at theruthexperience.com.